WISDOM

CHASER

Finding My Father at 14,000 Feet

NATHAN FOSTER

AFTERWORD BY RICHARD J. FOSTER

An imprint of InterVarsity Press
Downers Grove, Illinois

InterVarsity Press
P.O. Box 1400, Downers Grove, IL 60515-1426
World Wide Web: www.ivpress.com
E-mail: email@ivpress.com

InterVarsity Press® is the book-publishing division of InterVarsity Christian Fellowship/USA®, a
movement of students and faculty active on campus at hundreds of universities, colleges and schools
of nursing in the United States of America, and a member movement of the International Fellowship
of Evangelical Students. For information about local and regional activities, write Public Relations
Dept., InterVarsity Christian Fellowship/USA, 6400 Schroeder Rd., P.O. Box 7895, Madison, WI
53707-7895, or visit the IVCF website at <www.intervarsity.org>.

All Scripture quotations, unless otherwise indicated, are taken from the Holy Bible, New
International Version®. NIV®. Copyright ©1973, 1978, 1984 by International Bible Society. Used by
permission of Zondervan Publishing House. All rights reserved.

Design: Cindy Kiple
Images: Mt. Rainier: Philip Kramer/Getty Images

ISBN 978-0-8308-3630-7

Printed in the United States of America ∞

Library of Congress Cataloging-in-Publication Data

Foster, Nathan.
  Wisdom chaser: finding my father at 14,000 feet / Nathan Foster;
afterword by Richard J. Foster.
    p. cm.
  ISBN 978-0-8308-3630-7 (pbk.: alk. paper)
  1. Foster, Nathan. 2. Foster, Richard J. 3. Christian
biography—United States. 4. Fathers and sons—Religious
aspects—Christianity. 5. Mountaineering—Colorado. I. Title.
  BR1725.F5493A3 2010
  277.3'083092—dc22
    [B]

                                                            2009048958

P 22 21 20 19 18 17 16 15 14 13 12 11 10 9 8 7 6 5 4 3 2 1
Y 28 27 26 25 24 23 22 21 20 19 18 17 16 15 14 13 12 11 10

To Christy,

the depth of your beauty seems to know no bounds.

CONTENTS

1

IT NEVER HURTS TO ASK

My father loves the old adage "It never hurts to ask!" While I was growing up, he would often use the phrase with great enthusiasm—usually because he wasn't the one doing the asking.

The truth is that sometimes it *does* hurt to ask. In fourth grade I asked Krista Johnson to be my girlfriend, and she laughed in my face. In fifth grade, when I tried to kiss Becky Randall, she slapped me.

A few childhood experiences were all it took for me to lose my youthful candor. I learned my place in the world. I learned how to avoid the pain and hurt of rejection. I learned to stop asking.

But what does it cost us *not* to ask? Those consequences can be far worse. So one day I asked my father: "Hey Dad, you want to climb the highest mountain in Colorado?"

That simple question changed everything. Little did I know that attempting such a feat would be the easiest part of our journey.

In my mind, the question held only the risk involved in scaling a peak over fourteen thousand feet high, nearly three miles up in the air. Colorado has fifty-four such peaks, the most challenging and threatening summits in a state full of mountains. Every year, numerous people die on them, and even more are airlifted out. Search-and-rescue personnel stay busy in Colorado. In any given week they track people suffering from hypothermia or dehydration, people who have been hit by lightning or buried by avalanches, people who have fallen off mountainsides or who are just plain lost. Open any book on hiking in Colorado and you will encounter a series of standard warnings about sudden climate changes, dangerous afternoon storms, rock slides, bears, mountain lions, altitude sickness and even the potential danger of wearing cotton.

Coloradans are accustomed to news coverage about lost hikers and avalanche victims. But these stories were morbidly fascinating for a boy from Kansas, and perhaps a bit disheartening for his father. Maybe that was why he laughed in my face when I asked my question with such naive confidence.

"Yeah, right!" he bellowed out in great laughter. "We can't do that!" But I saw a twinge of interest in his eyes. My dad is forever the great dreaming pessimist, one of the many paradoxes about him that I have never understood. He was prepared to amuse his reckless son.

"No, Dad, I think we can," I countered. "I've got this book here." I held up *Dawson's Guide to Colorado's Fourteeners, Volume 1.* "Look; it's the complete mountaineering guide to Colorado's high peaks." The cover featured a photo of a weathered man standing on the edge of a snow-speckled cliff. My father did not share my recklessness, but both of us had a tendency to go after things that seemed just out of reach.

From time to time I got strange ideas about things I wanted to do, and I was stubborn about doing them whether they were feasible or not. In grade school I read a magazine ad about building a one-person helicopter from household appliances. I spent many a sleepless night fantasizing about parking my helicopter at the school bike rack.

In high school I read a book on how to live in the woods on pennies a day. For months I planned my Alaskan escape. I glued pictures of one-person forts inside of notebooks, and I dreamed of being a hermit, complete with creepy beard. This was my answer to failing grades and refusal to wear a tie.

I once decided that an old computer monitor would make a great fish tank. Inside the monitor I found a small tube with a note to call Poison Control if punctured. Who would have guessed that my experiment would result in a fire truck with lights and sirens blazing being sent to my house in the middle of the night? And that the truck would unload people encased in neon yellow toxic waste gear who would wave little beeping wands all around my garage? Or that my curious and confused neighbors would run outside in their robes and pajamas? By this time the firefighters knew me by name; this wasn't their first visit.

Some of my other plans were more viable, for better or worse. For example, my dream of living in a campground year-round actually came true—well, until my mouse-infested, Hantavirus death trap of a travel trailer ran out of heat in the dead of winter and my water froze while I was sick and vomiting everywhere with no phone in sight. This was my first near-death experience and the beginning of a major mouse phobia.

Family has a way of remembering these kinds of things. Dad was well acquainted with my history of grand plans, so I was careful when I approached him with the mountain-climbing idea. I made sure my mom and my wife were within earshot when I asked, because I knew their pessimism would only heighten his interest. My father tends to be level-headed and to play it safe, a tendency my mother is glad to reinforce. But I figured that the adventurer within him was longing for an opportunity to be set free. This could be his moment.

When I made my pitch, my mother shook her head on cue and my wife rolled her eyes. My father bit. We sat down at the kitchen table together—a twenty-two-year-old, two-pack-a-day smoker and his aging, out-of-shape father—paging through my new mountaineering guide. We both dared to ask: together, could we embark on an athletic feat of such magnitude?

◆   ◆   ◆

My father's experience with seeking what was beyond his reach had origins in his background of being orphaned, and consequently poverty stricken, in his late teens. Soon after multiple sclerosis ravaged his mother's health, his father died from emphysema. Dad's older brother was forced to take on the role of parent. Because they had no financial means to provide their mother with full-time medical care, the only way she could receive the help she needed was by admittance to a state-run mental institution, where she lived out the remainder of her days.

The summer of my father's high school graduation, he went on a mission trip, sponsored by a local Friends church, to help build a school for Native Alaskans. The school would be the first high school north of the Arctic Circle. One night, during the long drive from southern California up the Pacific coast, the van pulled into a small Oregon town. The lodging that night was the gymnasium floor at George Fox College. As my father lay there contemplating his future, he began dreaming of going to school full-time. This was an expensive proposition, and one that seemed completely out of his reach. In an unspoken prayer, he dared to ask the question: *Can I ever go to college? Can I ever go to* this *college?*

The trip was a promising one for my father, planting the seeds of much of his future life's work. But for now, the prospect of part-time night school at the local community college was all he could salvage of his dream. Full-time schooling was out of the question not only because of the expense but also because he was now expected to enter the labor force to ease the financial pressure on his older brother.

The first Friday after his return from Alaska, a local insurance company offered my dad a sales position. On Monday, he received news that a group of generous individuals was proposing to finance his college education. On Tuesday, with his brother's approval, he turned down the insurance job. The following Friday he was hitching a ride to Newberg, Oregon, to attend George Fox College.

That was one of the most important turning points in my father's life. It opened up new worlds to him, preparing him for the dreams he would continue to pursue in the years ahead. After all, he had learned that it never hurts to ask.

◆ ◆ ◆

For the first two decades of my life, I didn't really know my father. He was like a serious, silent ghost. My dad taught religion at a university, wrote books on spirituality and frequently spoke around the country. Occasionally I would accompany him to a place where he was speaking and observe strangers tearfully recounting how much his work had changed their life. My father didn't even know their names, but they felt an incredible connection with him. I didn't. The world seemed to know more of the man I grew up with than I did. I was the outsider.

Through the years, I grew fairly adept at keeping my distance from the whole family. My childhood was a jumble of emotions: guilt, fear, loneliness, longing and sometimes love. My dad was more like a mysterious icon than a full-fledged human being. When I was a kid, Dad would sometimes try to hug me. It made me so uncomfortable; I couldn't stand being touched. In my teens, our relationship had grown silent and hostile. When my parents punished me, they sometimes gave me the consequence of spending time with him, which was always awkward. As I became a young adult, my father and I seemed to have no time or interest in getting to know each other. We had nothing in common. The social glue was missing.

The strain of our unresolved arguments, and silence when words should have been spoken, had taken their toll. The distractions of life numbed my hurt, which over time hardened into apathy. Instead of respecting family members, I learned to tolerate them. The little I knew about my father I didn't much like. He and I learned how to be cordial with one another, and on occasion even managed to enjoy each other's company. But we didn't have any particular reason or opportunity to go beyond that. It would have been easy to drift into a pattern of visiting on the occasional holiday and calling a few times a year.

2

THE BEATING ON
MOUNT ELBERT

Our mountain adventure was planned. At 14,333 feet, Mount Elbert is the highest peak in the state of Colorado. The eastern route is over eleven miles, ascending 4,833 feet. *Dawson's Guide* indicated that the excursion would take nine hours round-trip. Although it sounds impressive, Elbert is actually one of Colorado's easier fourteeners to scale, requiring nothing technical. Yet the thought of its sheer magnitude impressed us both. Our challenge was set.

All of the literature about climbing a mountain of this height insists that a summit must be completed before noon, since nearly every afternoon dangerous lightning storms descend upon the peaks. This mandates a very early start. I hate getting up early; my father rises with the sun like clockwork. After a great deal of debate, we decided on a 5:30 a.m. start.

We bickered a bit about what we should take. Dad deferred to me as the expert, since I had skimmed part of a book and was able to talk confidently about what little knowledge I had. This, you will recognize, is the common criteria for leadership in our culture. Our expedition was no different.

We had an array of different foods, emergency overnight gear, winter storm attire and as much water as we could cram into our cheaply constructed backpacks that were designed for middle-schoolers. Dad's pack was blue with a neon "All Pro" patch proudly proclaiming his athleticism. Mine was black and not quite as embarrassing.

Then Dad got out his prized walking stick. Carved into its hilt was the image of an old man with a long beard blowing in the wind. It looked very cool—and horribly impractical. I pointed out that it probably weighed a good ten pounds, but Dad insisted on taking it. He would need it to fight off the bears, he said. This gave me free reign to pack a little luxury item myself. With much skill I secured a frothy bottle of Dr Pepper to the outside of my pack. I confess: I was an addict, and I enjoyed seeing my dad roar with hilarity at the ridiculousness of it.

My soda, his stick and our little-kid backpacks: we were set. On a cold June morning, two utter novices set out to brave the great unknown.

At the trailhead I rested against a tree in the dark, leisurely smoking a cigarette. I adopted the brave swagger of a veteran Air Force pilot before his greatest mission. My daydream was abruptly interrupted by my father's burst of laughter and the sight of him struggling to maintain his balance after strapping on his pack. We had failed to consider what it would be like to carry these packs; they were too heavy and uncomfortable for a day's journey. After discarding what we could—excluding the Dr Pepper and trusty walking stick—we ventured up the moonlit trail with a dawning realization of the torture ahead of us.

In some situations, all you can do is laugh—at least, all Dad could do was laugh, and occasionally comment on how he couldn't believe I had talked him into this. It was probably the ridiculous nature of this endeavor that made him giddy. I was serious; there was work to be done, goals to achieve. But his laughter, as it would many times later, helped maintain a sense of lightness about the whole event.

Bird song announced the arrival of the morning sun. The forest seemed filled with wonder and excitement. Witnessing the altering landscape as our elevation increased summoned our latent anticipation. Climate changes at such altitudes are remarkable. In June, you can just as easily expect snow as blistering heat. That day it was all heat.

By midmorning we had reached timberline. Unprotected by the high alpine forest, we hiked in open sun, which bore down on us with great intensity. I could see the trail meandering up the hill and around the bend, up and up and up. The heat of the sun at this altitude was merciless. It dried up our words to the briefest of exchanges.

"This sucks," I muttered to my father, gasping for air. He smiled and laughed a soft, strong laugh. Twenty steps later I continued my lament. "I don't know if I can make it," I said.

"Me neither," he smiled.

We were beaten, badly. My head throbbed in unison with my

rapidly beating heart. My legs ached like never before. I was dizzy from lack of oxygen. I felt truly miserable.

But as I looked back down the mountain, gauging our progress, a very odd thing happened: I fell in love with this kind of self-torture. Something about my wronged body suddenly began to feel right—the sensation was so raw and real. There we were in the thick of battle, two men fighting for every step. I had never felt this type of passion or intensity before. I was hooked. At the start, I don't believe either of us had really expected to summit that day. But the more we hiked, the more our challenge presented itself, and the more determined we became.

At last we reached the summit. We filled the thin air with joyous, exhausted laughter. I felt like a warrior from the days of old. Leaning proudly against his weathered hiking stick, my father sat in awe at our accomplishment. I sat on my torn backpack, slowly savoring my spoils: a ninety-degree Dr Pepper that never tasted better. As I had expected, I was overcome by the majesty of sitting on top of the world. What I didn't expect was to be moved by something much smaller. Vegetation on the top of a mountain of this height is a rare sight. At first glance, the mountainside looks rocky and dusty, but as I took a closer look, an ecological wonder unfolded. Nestled in the cracks of the rocks grew a miniature world of plant life. There were miniscule flowers everywhere, arrayed in purple, yellow and blue. How anything grows in such a harsh climate is beyond me. Equally stunning is how easily such beauty can be missed. I had been staring at the ground out of sheer exhaustion and had simply stumbled across this flora wonderland. What I didn't notice was that a shift between father and son had begun.

◆   ◆   ◆

From my vantage point at the start of our climb on that June day, far too early in the morning for humans to be awake, I had seen my father and me as polar opposites. As we worked our way up the hot and dusty trail, however, I began to see similarities between us. The harder the task, the more we both wanted it. Two things were clear: we were both badly out of shape, and we were both scrappy, stubborn fighters. I had known my own propensity to fight, but I had not known my father's, and it greatly surprised me. This was the same man who would marvel at flowers all day long, the praying pacifist who wore gloves whenever there was work to do.

Somewhere in the haze of our strenuous activity, I remembered a day from the past. After not being allowed to attend my best friend's birthday party, I had thrown the biggest fit of my life. I remember standing on my bed, screaming at Dad. He countered me, doing the stern father thing, and we went back and forth, fighting for power. Then my father did the strangest thing: he knelt down and closed his eyes. This act enraged me all the more. I demanded that he get up and fight me, but his only posture was silence. What was he doing? Was he being weak? Shutting me out? I didn't understand it, but eventually it stopped the fight.

That event had left me feeling two distinct things: ashamed for the way I had behaved and deeply moved by my dad's action. That day on the side of the windy mountain, I was moved by him once again. I looked over at him and noticed the sweat pouring from his brow, the shaking of his calves from the strain. He was a fighter. I saw strength in my father, and it was beautiful.

Now I dared to ask myself the question: *Have I been wrong about who my father is?*

❖ ❖ ❖

The irony of climbing a fourteener is that just when you are celebrating the accomplishment of having made it to the top, you have to turn around and go back down the way you came. This can be a cruel and methodical process. The trip down is much easier cardiovascularly, but physically it held a new set of challenges. My legs, weak from the journey, often buckled as I pounded out thousands of steps.

As we reversed direction to return to the trailhead, I began to think about what was facing me after this triumphant climb. I was returning to a lot of uncertainty. My twenty-two years of life as a relative failure haunted me. It seemed that I failed at everything I tried, the most notable being school. After dropping out of high school, I had served brief stints of marginal ruin at four different colleges. Finally, after spending a week laboring over my one-page application essay, I had been accepted into Colorado State University and was planning to study social work in the coming months. Thank God for provisional admission status.

It is an understatement to say that I was feeling uncertain about my ability to succeed in college. More accurately, I was terrified. I was motivated by the horror of a thousand countless hours of mind-numbing labor in crappy jobs I had endured. I had to do this. There was an unfulfilled longing boiling up in me from deep inside, and it refused to be ignored. I *had* to do this.

Could my internal churning possibly be what my dad had felt at the prospect of ignoring his dreams and instead working in insurance for the rest of his life? At fourteen thousand feet, the distance between two poles has a funny way of shrinking.

Descending Mount Elbert, I could hardly believe that in just two months I would once again be facing my own personal insur-mountable peak: college. I was headed back to a painful, failure-ridden environment. I was being given another chance, but I as-sumed that it would be my last. What would I make of it?

Questions danced in my tired mind. Exhilarated by our success on Mount Elbert, I began voicing them to myself: *Can I actually finish college? Can I quit smoking? Can I stay sober? Can I become someone? Can I get to know the old man with the walking stick?*

During that long trek down, on one of the proudest days of my life, I began dreaming of things that had previously seemed out of reach. My father's words echoed in my head: *It never hurts to ask.*

3

THE QUANDARY OF DREAMING

DREAMING IS A GIFT FEW PEOPLE POSSESS. Well-intentioned teachers and parents will caution children to get their heads out of the clouds (never mind the fact that we are made in the image of the ultimate Creator). Once we work the creative dreams out of our children, we send them into a world ready to sell them shallow, socially acceptable dreams—three easy payments and thirty days to riches, relationships or rock-solid abs.

Dreaming was easy for me, probably due to my rebellious nature. Our success on Mount Elbert lit a deep fervor for mountain exploration. I spent the following winter dreaming of the next summer's mountain excursions, purchasing books and maps and selecting hiking gear. I pursued the hiking of fourteeners with the passion of an addict. Dreaming required very little mental and emotional risk; the real question was whether I could learn to follow through and actually do the work.

I have been wounded enough to understand the complex process of verbalizing one's dream. Our world is chock-full of individuals who have dreamed and failed. Worse yet are the people who have beaten fate to the punch and never even allowed themselves to hope. I've met many people who sell the secret excuses and lies they tell themselves. You can feel the passive stabs behind their practical advice: "I could never do anything like that." "You just have to know the right people." "It's so competitive out there." What they are all subconsciously saying is, "I can't be anything more, and so certainly you can't either. Won't you please validate my fear of failure?" Failure leeches can come in handy, of course; spite has motivated me many times.

Encouragement, however, is a far greater motivator. My wife is one of those people who will confidently tell me I am capable of doing things I would not otherwise consider. Her encouragement remains a significant driving force behind everything I have attempted to do. This type of optimism can work against me, of course, when it comes to cleaning the kitchen.

◆　◆　◆

I learned as a small child that I needed to take great caution before broaching an idea or plan with my father. He was a far cry from a failure leech, but his pessimism could make him an unsettling person to talk to. Timing and mood were of utmost importance.

Dad was in the habit of being horribly practical—always rooting for the underdog yet holding fast to the improbability of victory. I must have learned this practice from him, because I do the same, except I tend to believe the least favored competitor can actually win. My father, on the other hand, will remain pessimistic until the very end. Dad will actually roll on the floor laughing in surprise when an underdog team pulls off a victory. His antics have even resulted in a foot injury that required surgery years later. Some men have bad knees from playing football; my dad has a chronic spectator sprain.

Although he cares little about sports, my dad follows the NCAA college basketball tournament with great enthusiasm, as no other event seems to yield more victories for unfavored teams. He once told me that he had a sporting fantasy. "Nate," he said softly, as if beginning a confession, "I've always had this fantasy that I was a basketball player who couldn't make a basket to save his life."

"That's no fantasy. That's reality!" I snapped back.

"Okay. Okay," he smiled, impressed with my cleverness. Deprecation is a value in my family.

"Here's the rub," he went on. "I could only do one thing: steal the ball." His voice shifted to a strong, slow whisper. "Anytime I wanted to, I could steal the ball. Out of nowhere I would come . . ." I later learned that this is my dad: the little guy no one expected anything from who came out of nowhere.

This underdog phenomenon plays out between me and my father. Maybe I'm overcompensating for past failures, but I tend to believe few things are out of my reach if I get motivated enough to really apply myself. My dad had very few expectations of me; he saw me as a sort of underdog and always seemed surprised when I accomplished anything. I never really cared to prove much to my dad, but I did want him to believe in me. I think he wanted to believe in me as well. I would find myself finishing tasks just to prove they could be done. In the end, I shared very few dreams with my dad—at least not until I had my ideas exceptionally well-planned. I wouldn't have dared to tell him that I wanted to climb *all* of the fourteeners in Colorado. I don't know that I would want to now.

But I was dreaming big. Secretly I was plotting out the years it would take to summit all of Colorado's fifty-four highest peaks. Dreams became plans. That summer we would summit seven fourteen-thousand-foot mountains. I didn't really know what I was doing, yet my father seemed to trust me.

As I was finishing my first year at Colorado State, I had dreams of conquering other kinds of mountains. My nervousness and doubt about college had proven to be well-founded; it was tough. But I worked hard and did fairly well. Every day that year I biked to school, and this became my prayer time. I'm sure I looked like a mad man talking and yelling out loud as I pedaled on. While riding though a heavy rain one summer day, I saw a vision of myself as a nonsmoker. My prayers had produced an insatiable desire to stop smoking, and I was instantly struck with an un-yielding curiosity. I felt like a child dreaming of Christmas. Drunk with a rush of anticipation, I could hardly wait to see who I would become.

This dream was big. One of my greatest joys in life was smok-ing. Nicotine had always walked me through hard times; it was a friend I had visited up to forty times per day for the last ten years.

I quit smoking with great drama and diligence, recording my progress with video diaries. Take one: "This isn't going to be too hard. I know I can do this!" Take two: "It's harder than I thought it would be, but I can handle it." Take three (five hours later in fetal position and pulling my hair): "@#$%^%$!"

◆　◆　◆

A week into the nonsmoking madness, I was ready to test my new lungs on Mount Quandary. Dad and I arrived near the base of this appropriately named peak just as dusk was setting in. From a long and winding highway, we got our first glimpses of the next day's torture. Quandary was a beautiful mountain with a gentle ridge expanding to the sky. We could see soft patches of snow through the fog and haze of the setting sun. It was cold, and the wind rushed about as I quickly snapped a few photos.

"Are you ready for tomorrow?" Dad asked with a smile and a hint of disbelief at our task.

"I'm ready to crawl out of my skin!" I said as I spit a sunflower seed shell from my mouth. "Seven days without a smoke. I need a mountain. I need something."

"Well, keep going, kid," he said smiling, completely surprised at my progress.

Night fell as we navigated to the trailhead. We journeyed down a ravine and set up the tent by flashlight. Sitting by a fire, we recounted the recent happenings of our lives. My lack of nicotine and my insistence on taking everything out on those around me must have made for unpleasant company. My wife and I had been fighting constantly, and this trip was a welcome release. Dad is as skilled as they come with handling the foul moods of others. It was good to be with him.

Quandary was a shorter climb than most mountains. After much persuading and repeated counting aloud in order to prove we had enough time, I got my dad to agree on an 8:00 a.m. start. "So set the alarm for 6:30, Nate," Dad stated firmly.

"Six-thirty! You're mad! The trail is right up that hill. I'll sleep in my clothes. Seven forty-five will do just fine," I barked.

Dad burst into an off-tune song as he folded his socks, "My son doesn't like to get up early. Doo a la la la. Don't you know the early bird gets the worm? [He always quoted old parables.] Doo a la la la. My son wants to sleep all day. La la la."

I smiled and drifted off to sleep.

I've never been good at waking up. As a teenager I had been known to have crazy—sometimes even violent—morning episodes, most of which I would have no memory of. It was common knowledge in my family that I wouldn't talk for at least a good half hour upon waking. I would occasionally grunt, but I was incapable of conversation. My dad found my reluctance to join the living as odd and a bit amusing. It almost seemed as if he found pleasure in pushing my limits. Yet in the end he usually respected my limitations and quietly waited for my full consciousness.

Before my alarm went off, I heard that ridiculous tune outside the tent. Dad was reading a book with a wild, energetic look about him. As promised, I emerged from my sleeping bag fully dressed, strapped on my boots, hoisted on my backpack and headed for the trail. Dad smiled as if he had something funny to say, but with keen discernment he just followed. The trail was damp and hazy, and somehow reflective of my state of mind. My thoughts turned to our first mountain summit the preceding summer, and I recalled the personality characteristics I had discovered in my father on that journey.

On the mountain I had seen a different side of my father than I had known growing up. Maybe he changed or was changing. Maybe I was changing. I was noticing the hint of a rebellious side to him. I kind of liked this guy.

Dad was now light and fun to be around. I was serious, driven and cranky. He was supposed to be the somber one. What had happened? Had I taken on the characteristics that I disliked in my father? While I was growing up, Dad's ghostly presence usually brought an air of seriousness, like a barely visible wind—gentle, quiet and empty. Coming and going. Doing what he needed to do around the house and with the family, then drifting off into his office. During my grade school years, I often thought my father seemed kind of sad. I don't remember him talking much. He would quietly creep out from his office when a problem occurred, but otherwise it always seemed like he had something to do. He was never really rushed or stressed, yet he was always working. Dad had a multitude of speaking opportunities—most he passed on, but many he accepted.

As the years went by, it seemed I saw less and less of my father and cared less and less about his absence. At some point I shifted from wanting him to be home, counting down the days to when he would return, and eagerly greeting him at the airport, to not knowing when he was gone or home and caring even less.

As a child, I was proud of my dad. Hearing him speak to crowds filled me with excitement; perhaps he would mention my name, or tell a story about me, or in some way acknowledge his home life. At first I think I accepted that God was using my dad to help people. Later I felt mildly ambivalent about the fact that God seemed to need my dad. Somewhere along the way, my feelings shifted to embarrassment and anger that Dad had "holier work" to do. By thirteen I was filled with rage, and I shut down.

Granted, much of my experience was normal development, but a deep wound was formed. The fruits of my childhood were bitterness and disgust for anything Christian. I'm not foolish enough to overlook how a child's reality and the truth of a situation can often be miles apart. Yet that was my experience—right or wrong, correct or incorrect. Those were the feelings that remained with me.

When children feel unpleasant emotions, seem to have an innate tendency to blame themselves. Maybe it's the self-absorbed nature of childhood; maybe it's just some misplaced guilt from the Fall. But now, climbing Mount Quandary, I was past completely blaming myself for my own childhood. Maybe it was Quandary's mountain air, but my disdain had calmed. The intense rage had turned to mild ambivalence. I was becoming aware that my dad really didn't know how to be a father and that I didn't know how to be a son. On this journey, both of us were lost.

◆ ◆ ◆

Doesn't God wish to give us the desires of our hearts, looking for every opportunity to bless without destroying us in the process? I was discovering the problem was not with my ability to dream, but with my heart. What if my dreams weren't so self-centered and instead were truly altruistic? What if I dreamed of grace and giving, of small, simple things suited to my finite capacities?

His eyes blazing with desire, a pastor friend once described to me the plan of growth he wanted for his church. I told him he should try something more altruistic, such as dreaming of growth for the church across town, the one he secretly competed with. My call to selflessness went unappreciated. Altruistic or not, my dreams are relatively useless unless I'm willing and able to do my part of the work.

We were less than halfway up Quandary and I was unimpressed with my new lungs. I was working like I did last summer on Elbert: hiking as hard and fast as I could until I keeled over with exhaustion. Moments later I would rip myself from the comfort of a cold rock and proceed with diminished enthusiasm. This was misery.

4

FINDING MY PACE ON
MOUNT QUANDARY

DAD ONCE TOLD ME THE STORY of a Chinese calligrapher teaching others his art. He sent the students home to draw lines between the words of an entire newspaper. At the second lesson he told his students to repeat the first lesson for the next year. If they worked really hard for an entire year, only then might they be ready to learn how to draw a letter.

This type of education would never work in our results-obsessed culture. I've learned well how to orchestrate my days by racing from task to task. I get up and do all I can as quickly as possible, only to start again the follow day. I remain too busy to really invest in anyone else. Where did I get the idea that slow equals bad?

"Nate, I think if we move at a really slow pace, we won't have to stop as often. Here, watch." My father moved his feet methodically, slow but steady.

"Dad, you're crazy!" I laughed. "We'll never get there! Look how slow you're walking. I could crawl faster. You look ridiculous!"

"Do what you want," he muttered. "I'm going to walk slowly!"

I brushed off my father's wisdom and raced ahead up the mountain. After about a half hour of hiking up a steep pitch, I noticed that, with all my painful stops, he was keeping up with me. I felt exhausted. Dad didn't stop even once, and he seemed to be gliding up the mountain.

As is often the case in life, pain made me teachable. That day it was burning lungs and shaky legs. My father had a lesson to teach about hard work, and I was ready to learn. I gave Dad's theory a try and joined his ridiculously slow march. I soon discovered that if I kept going slowly, it was easier not to stop. I couldn't believe it. There on the side of the mountain, one of my lifelong quandaries was being revealed. The answer was just so simple.

Pace yourself.

Move slowly.

Don't stop.

This turned out to be an ingenious way to climb a mountain. If I know my limits and am willing to accept them, all I have to do is keep moving forward. Dream big and find my pace.

Eventually we summited with grace and precision and a slow, steady pace. The destination proved more remarkable than I had remembered from our last climb.

With blurry vision and cloudy thoughts, I gazed upon mountain after mountain poised against the horizon. I was dirty, tired and proud. My head throbbed in pain; my legs were swollen and useless. I took a bruised apple from my pack and bit in. It tasted delicious.

I glanced over at my warrior father. He never came across to me as particularly bright or clever, but what he lacked in knowledge he made up for in hard work. Apparently my dad was never much of a student. He was the kid who studied constantly and still got Cs. Dad seemed to have some natural understanding of some topics, but of others he certainly didn't. All my life I had watched my writer-father work diligently, trying to learn high school grammar and sentence structure. It always seemed odd that, as a writer, he couldn't spell basic words. I knew that if I needed help spelling a word I shouldn't ask Dad, because he wouldn't know. He would take the time to practice the forgotten art of looking up a word in the dictionary with me, but it was usually quicker to just ask my mom or brother.

It's really no wonder that Dad had discovered this great way to hike up steep elevations. In one sense this is the way he lived his life. It seemed to always take Dad forever to complete a task. I once heard my father quote a famous writer who said he had spent all morning deciding whether or not to use a comma and then all afternoon deciding whether to take it out. This was more a reality than a joke. My dad has been an author for nearly thirty years, and he has only five books to show for it. Some writers put out a book every year. "Anything worth doing is worth doing well," he would say whenever the opportunity arose.

As a child, I must have driven my dad nuts. He always attempted to do things the right way, regardless of how much labor and precision a task required. I, on the other hand, usually looked for the easy way out. "The quicker the better" was my motto. I cut every corner I could find, making up a few as I went. The results didn't always turn out the way I wanted. I was ready to learn a new way to approach tasks.

Sitting on top of the mountain, it became wonderfully clear to me how the idea of pacing fit into my smoke-free journey. How do I quit smoking? One slow, methodical step at a time.

Relax.

Slow down.

Live each moment.

I had been busy holding my breath, attacking a smoke-free life with all the enthusiasm and gusto I could muster. I was too consumed with fighting to live the process. Without pacing, hard work is wasted. I now saw that few things were beyond my reach as long as I took my time.

The whole notion of pacing myself was so simple, yet it sparked a revolution, a cosmic shift in the way in which I attempted to live my life. My string of failures was about to end. I was learning how to hike. I was learning how to live from a man I had determined had nothing to teach me.

❖　❖　❖

A black cloud was rapidly moving across the sky, cutting short my daydreams. Our elevation was not conducive to greeting the mystery of the storm moving in. The rain was of no concern; in fact, it would be a welcome test of my new gear and would heighten the drama of our experience. It was the thought of seeing dazzling flashes of light that motivated our steady departure.

We were nearly down the mountain when the thunder summoned the storm. The rain fell hard, exposing the weakness in my newly acquired paraphernalia. We nestled under a tree and sat in awe.

◆   ◆   ◆

Around 2:00 p.m. we staggered back to camp wet, cold and terribly exhausted. I crawled into the tent and fell asleep. The next thing I remember is my dad sitting up with a ridiculous smile on his face and muttering something about the town of Idaho Springs and Beau Jo's.

For the benefit of those outside of Colorado: to say that Beau Jo's is a pizza place is like saying the pope is just some religious guy. My mother is very sensitive about the types of food my father consumes. Concerned for his digestion, she always packs him a medley of pills. I seldom remember my father getting excited about much of anything, but the mention of two things could always incite a mild frenzy: pizza and Mexican food. The forbidden fare.

This day, my father's illicit longing was for the crown jewel of pizzas. From his sleepy calculations, we could be at Beau Jo's in a couple of hours, marking a memorable end to our Quandary experience.

From the highway I glanced back at Mount Quandary in my rearview. The old saying that time heals all wounds just wasn't true. Rather, time makes wounds more tolerable. It eases the sting. We can't go back and relive our lives; we can't change the past. We do, however, have some say in the future. I wondered what else the old man had to teach me.

5

TIME
LOVE'S ALLEGORY

"HOW WAS THE TRIP?" my wife asked eagerly as she greeted my broken body at the door.

"Good. We summited in four and half hours. We made good time."

My thoughts drifted. Why does the speed at which I travel make the time "good"? What does it say about me and my priorities that I ascribe good and bad traits based on the speed at which I travel?

After an odd moment of silence, I eagerly rejoined the conversation. "I learned how to pace myself."

"Well, it's about time," she playfully muttered, with a sense of hopelessness.

"What?" I asked.

"Oh yeah, you always get ticked off when things don't go according to your schedule." Her frustration was obvious. I had scratched a wound. There's nothing quite like marriage to reveal our shortcomings. It just might be that few people really care enough to tell us the truth about ourselves.

In a soft tone, with sincere interest, Christy took a chance. "Just what is it you're in such a hurry to do?"

I searched for the answer. "I don't know. More important things, I guess."

Christy instantly replied, as if the conversation had been rehearsed. "What is more important than spending time with others?"

I looked down in silence and thought to myself, "Maybe I mean more enjoyable things." *Oh, there you are, selfishness, my old friend. You're behind this matter. I should have known.*

❖ ❖ ❖

After finding my pace on Quandary, my love affair with the outdoors was in full bloom. Virtually every other weekend that summer, Dad and I did something together. We climbed mountains and took afternoon trips to outdoor stores. We day hiked in a canyon near Dad's house and whitewater rafted in the river near mine. For the first time, Dad and I had something to talk about on the phone.

All of my life I have loved the mountains. Much of my life I have had masochistic tendencies. Who knew the two could blend together so well? I saw the pain of climbing mountains as a therapeutic beating. My father did not see mountains the same way.

When I was with my dad, he almost always had this strange look in his eyes, a sort of disconnected contentedness. Sitting in afternoon traffic or summiting a peak: it seemed to make little difference to my dad. He appeared at peace in each situation. I, on the other hand, lived on extremes. One minute completely irritated and frustrated, the next happy and full of hope, like a rapid-cycling bipolar. If I was doing what I wanted to do, I was as content as a Zen master. If life didn't go exactly as I had planned, I was an ass.

❖   ❖   ❖

Early that August, Dad and I hiked Mount Sherman, a relatively easy and isolated fourteener. It was a barren climb almost the entire way, far from the lushness of Mount Quandary. In the scorching sun we nestled in a cove of rocks on the summit. It was hot and dusty. I was tired and cranky. Today my sandwich was soggy, and my warm Dr Pepper had lost its novelty. I was already thinking of the next conquest.

"Nate, see that mountain?" Dad said. "It has a stunning ridge. That's a perfectly good peak. If it stood a few feet higher, you would know its name and want to climb it. As it stands, it's an unnamed mountain that no one bothers with." Dad knew I was uninterested in mountains under fourteen thousand feet. He saw value in the things that others disregarded. I did not.

I had no time for his playful observation. Map in hand, I scouted the horizon for other fourteeners. Moments later I heard chuckling nearby. On the east side of the summit was a patch of snow nestled in a small crevasse, and there was the old man, rolling around with glee. With the innocence and vulnerability of a child who didn't want to play alone, he motioned me to join. I reluctantly decided to make an attempt at fun. That afternoon we shaved a good two hundred and fifty feet off of our descent by sliding down the snow. Both entertained and apprehensive, Dad screeched and hollered the whole way down.

The fact that we had reached the summit seemed to matter little to my dad. To me it was everything. Every time I stood atop a mountain peak it was a marker, a triumph, an erosion of my sense of failure. I did something. I set a goal, worked hard and achieved success. In the caverns of my mind, worth and value were being fashioned all because I could climb a mountain. Pretty shallow, I know; yet it seemed a better way to shape an identity than the cultural alternatives of work, money and sexual prowess.

◆   ◆   ◆

Wandering down the trail, I glanced over at Dad. He smiled with affirmation. My thoughts began to wander. How do we know when we are loved? Is it that look of acceptance, a smile and warm embrace? Or is it when someone buys us crap we don't need or lets us have our own way? The ultimate expression of love has to be taking a bullet for someone, losing your life so someone else can live. You know, the Jesus way. A heroic stranger sacrifices her own life to save that of a child about to be struck down by a wayward semi. Our heroine just gave the child what potential time on earth she had left so that the kid could have more. Minus the possible pain, dying for someone is giving them a lot of potential time. When we share our time, is this not the pinnacle of human sacrifice?

Time lets us know that we are loved. In periods of isolation or sadness when someone shares their time, it doesn't just mean a lot—it means everything. The only thing I have any control over is what I do in this fleeting moment. Time, my most valuable possession, is quite possibly my only real possession.

Isn't one illustration of God's love the offering of his constant presence to us? Even still, my struggle to show up for others remains. What does it say when I withhold this valuable commodity? Busyness is the ultimate trump card. It will get you out of virtually every social situation, or at least buy you amnesty a few times when you let a friend down. "I'm so sorry I forgot your birthday. I've just been so busy."

It's also the excuse we use when we've really screwed up. Sprinkle a little religious babble into the verbiage and the guilt just washes away. "Sorry I didn't call when you were in the hospital. I just have so much going on right now. I know you thought you were going to die and had reached the depths of helplessness when you were unable to wipe your own ass. But I'm sure God will work all this out for the best. I'll be praying for you."

If I'm busy, I don't have to be responsible for what I fail to do. Yet my actions send a message whether I intend them to or not. Of course, it's probably no coincidence that most people set up a life of near panic. Like any other addiction, busyness works so well. It gives us the edge to avoid emptiness, loneliness, unpleasant memories, hurt, intimacy—and, subsequently, the clarity that silence and an unhurried life can bring. Still, almost everyone I know is trying to get caught up, trying to commit to fewer things, and aching to get away from the frantic race that consumes modern America. Self included. Truth is, sometimes I don't want a slow-paced, intentional life. I have systematically engineered a life of chaos. The consequences at least appear better than facing the reality of my own life. And so each generation is more disconnected than the last. When I look around at the world, I see a bunch of people desperate to know they are loved living in the shadows of a community too busy to pay attention to anyone but themselves. Maybe we shouldn't be surprised when the school guidance counselor commits suicide or a baby is found in a dumpster. A kid who shoots his classmates knows nothing of love.

Dad and I meandered our way back to the car. In contentedness and silence I drove home. Here I was, spending all this time with my dad. My motivations were thrill and accomplishment. What were his? He didn't care about accomplishments. He was content reading an ancient book and falling asleep in front of the TV watching some old musical. Why was he climbing these giant mountains with his temperamental son? The answer was right in front of me, yet it would take years for me to discover.

6

FREEDOM TO FAIL

FOR YEARS I HAD DOUBTED MY ABILITY to do much more than fake and cheat my way through life. Deep down I knew I just couldn't cut it. Lies about my lack of ability, inferior intelligence and poor social graces had been the background music of my life. But now the song was changing. My successes at college and on the mountains were leading me to a new lie. I was now "The Shit."

In *Mere Christianity,* C. S. Lewis writes this great line about pride: "If you think you are not conceited, it means you are very conceited indeed." In order to prove how distorted I am, I will share with you my thoughtful response to Lewis.

Dear Jack,

You're the man. Those lion stories are top-notch. The Space Trilogy was brilliantly sneaky, and *Till We Have Faces* is the best book ever written. You have a knack for making the hidden obvious. But your thoughts on pride, well, you really missed the mark on that one. I'm sure it's hard to be humble when you've been a professor at both Oxford and Cambridge. The thing is, Mr. Lewis, you just don't know me. I could line up a dozen respectable witnesses to testify to my humility. Pride has never been an issue for me. Rage, jealousy and lust, yeah: I got them all and probably a few more. But not pride.

Sincerely,
Nathan Foster

I had adopted the arrogant and confident stride of a person who truly hates himself. Low self-esteem and arrogant pride are just different sides of the same coin. Both creatures live and die by one's success or failure.

Little did I know that pride was the root of my shortcomings. Take a beaten-up person, add a splash of success, and a monster is born. Arrogance had burrowed its way in. At my greatest moments of self-absorption, I was completely unaware of its cunning nature. Even so, the mountains were ready to put me in my place as an utter novice. It's almost humorous how quickly I got a big head. Out of deep-seated self-disdain rose a beast. Mine was about to be beaten down.

Secretly I was beginning to wonder why some people didn't summit every mountain they attempted. So far I was a perfect seven for seven. It's just like me to take a small sample and extend it into everything else. I had learned that pain and exhaustion were manageable conditions. As far as I was concerned, I really couldn't think of a legitimate reason not to summit—save lightning, of course. Hiking in a storm was just stupid. Lightning kills more people each year in the United States than rattlesnakes, black widows, brown recluse spiders, mountain lions, bears, wolves, scorpions, centipedes, alligators, sharks and dogs combined.

◆　◆　◆

I had always loved the mountains and everything about them. The decision to move to Colorado was a compromise with my wife. I wanted to live in the Northwest; she wanted to be a day's drive from her family in Kansas. It was a bonus that my parents lived in Colorado. But the real deciding factor happened during a beer with Mark, a transplant to Colorado from the Midwest, when he told me about hiking Longs Peak: "I thought I was going to die. My heart raced and my head pounded. I couldn't walk for a week after attempting to summit Longs Peak."

I was clearly enticed.

"It's really a serious endeavor," Mark patiently stated.

I was sold. The next day we signed a lease, and three months later we were attaching those beautiful green Colorado tags to my truck. So when Dad and I first started attacking fourteeners, Longs was the mountain I wanted. However, Mark's statements and my trusty guidebook had convinced me that I needed to work my way up to Longs.

Longs is a popular peak. Hence the stories abounded, as did my angst about scaling it. I ate literally hundreds of lunches seated on a bench, staring at Longs. I sat mesmerized by its prominent presence. Lunch would usually end with me cursing at the mountain, for I knew its challenge was formidable. But I wanted my chance. My boots had now treaded on seven fourteen-thousand-foot summits. I was ready.

A summit up Longs requires trekking five thousand feet into the sky. It would take us a good fourteen hours of nonstop work to cover the fifteen-mile journey. Its name doesn't derive from its length, however. Rather, in 1820 Stephen Long wrote about seeing the mountain; for this deed, it bears his name. It was only in an obscure book that I learned that Native peoples had a lengthy history of catching bald eagles on the summit. You know the old story: white man comes along and suddenly the mountains are "discovered."

Longs Peak was still intimidating, despite my heightened sense of mountaineering abilities. Through reading and local conversation, I learned that near the crest of the summit is a narrow ledge in what is known as the "Trough." From what I could ascertain, crossing this ledge requires crawling for roughly thirty feet. The ledge is apparently two feet wide, with a sheer one-thousand-foot drop as a reward for those who have not yet mastered their crawling skills. As if that weren't enough, the Trough is nestled under a ledge that receives virtually no sunlight, so it remains covered in ice for all but a week or two in late summer. My only hope lay in a small window of time between the melting of the ice and the early fall snowstorms. This two-week window changes from year to year, making it impossible to know just when the ice has melted. So basically you're crawling on a narrow ledge, on ice, with no railing, and if you fall, you're dead. Of course, this was the easiest route up the peak. Every year people die on Longs, thus only deepening its allure. The mere thought of the Trough literally caused my palms to sweat. I would lie in bed and envision crawling on ice through this narrow ledge, desperately trying to picture a positive outcome. Sometimes I wished I hadn't read about the climbs and had just gone blindly up like so many others. Dad wasn't interested in doing any ice crawling, but he was at least willing to go and check things out.

"Now Nate, you need to know that I'm not going to do anything stupid up there. If I don't like the way it looks, you're on your own, buddy!" Dad told me resolutely.

"Anything stupid?" I fired back. "You mean like getting up at 2:00 in the morning and hiking in the dark? Or do you mean the fourteen hours of nonstop hiking, three-fourths of which is uphill?" Humor was my usual weapon when Dad was serious.

It was true. In order to summit by noon, we had to start at 2:00 a.m. The first four hours of the hike were to be done in the dark with the aid of headlamps. How to get sleep before embarking on this grueling adventure was a dilemma. Dad's solution was to arrive at the base in the afternoon and go to sleep by 5:00 p.m. I had to work that day and couldn't arrive until 7:00 or 8:00 p.m., so my solution was to get jacked up on caffeine and pull an all-nighter. Over the phone we bickered about what seemed like an unworkable situation. In the end, we both stuck to our own plan. In the end, neither solution was viable.

"Just meet me at the Longs Peak campground in Rocky Mountain National Park, site seventeen, by 2:00 a.m.," Pops gruffly stated.

Dad was always clear about the details. I was the one who had found the campground and had determined the time to meet, yet he was sure to repeat these details back to me as if they were his information.

"I'll be sleeping while you're out doing whatever," he snapped with a tone that was both playful and conclusive.

I finished work, packed up my truck and ventured out as the

sun was beginning to disappear. The night air rushed against my face as I sped through Big Thompson Canyon. "Winds of change," I thought idly. My father had spent a mysterious winter living in this canyon when he was ten. Apparently when my dad was a child, my grandfather had to move around frequently to look for work. My father had some distant relative who owned a summer cabin in this narrow and isolated canyon, so his family moved there for a winter. Dad always smiles when he talks about that season. While it was a desperate attempt at survival for his family, it was sheer delight for my father. Dad would eagerly recount to me the long winter without school and the vast canyon at his fingertips. He especially lit up when he talked of falling asleep in front of a wood-burning stove, the only source of heat for the dilapidated cabin. To this day, sleeping in front of a fire remains one of his greatest pleasures. There are defining moments in childhood that forge our interests and passions. Amid the rocks and woods of Big Thompson Canyon, my father fell in love with the natural world. That night I thought of the little boy who had explored these encompassing walls.

The stars graced the edges of the spiral canyon. The air had a strange quality about it, choking and yet somehow refreshing. I felt as if I was driving to my death. I was ready to die. My life was good, solid and complete. You know how in some old Western films the Indian sniffs the air and confidently mutters about the weather? Well, the air was like that. I just wasn't the confident Indian I should have been. I had never smelled what I would soon discover.

The moon was well on its way to the crest of the sky by the time I arrived at site seventeen at the Longs Peak campground in Rocky Mountain National Park. With the aid of a flashlight, I tried with great effort to pitch my tent. Strong gusts of wind kept ripping it out of my hands. Setting up a tent in strong wind by yourself is impossible. This was either going to be incredibly frustrating or a moment of great hilarity. We have those choices in life. This time I did what my dad would have done, and probably did do in the previous hours. I jumped on my flopping tent, wrestled it to the ground and burst into laughter.

"Nate, you're early. Party already over?" Dad said from his own tent.

"What happened to your seven hours of beauty sleep?" I bantered back.

"This blasted wind. It's so noisy. I can't sleep!" Dad stated with frustration and amazement.

"Imagine that! You couldn't sleep at five o'clock in the evening. Who knew?"

"Oh stop it, Nate. The wind is so noisy."

"Right, Dad. Right. Since you're awake and all, what do you think about giving me a hand out here?"

"Where were you when I wrestled my tent?" Dad fired back.

"At work," I stammered.

"Kids these days, they don't . . ."

"Yeah, yeah, yeah. Come give me a hand." Dad came out of his tent wide awake.

I will never forget lying in the tent that night. The wind was howling in a way I had never imagined possible. I thought surely the tent would blow away, taking me with it in a sort of Wizard of Oz re-creation. Keep in mind that I grew up in Kansas: I knew wind. I knew tornados, but this was different. Dad was right; the noisy wind made sleeping nearly impossible. Just when I would start to drift off, a gust would howl an eerie tune. I would jolt awake and quickly open my eyes, making sure I hadn't left the campsite. It didn't help that I was obsessed with the icy Trough. The thought of wind on the icy Trough was more than I could bear.

"The wind has to die down at some point," I whispered.

Occasionally, a muffled bellow of laughter would come from my father's tent. Less occasionally Dad would yell from his tent the predictable question, "Nate, are you sure you want to do this?"

There was no need to answer. He knew what I would say. By moonlight, I was staring at my watch as it switched from 1:59 to 2:00. "Beep! Beep!" The pointless sound was muffled by the wind.

"You ready for this?" I said to myself, trying to sound confident and encouraging.

Leaving the warm safety of my sleeping bag and venturing into the black whirling abyss, I was both frightened and exhilarated. The best joys in life usually have an embedded element of fear: your wedding day, the first day at an important job, the day your child is born. Today felt like one of those days.

We arose from our tents that late summer morning bundled in Arctic gear. We exchanged smiles, fully aware of the insanity we were pursuing. We were like boys hunting for treasure. It was cold, dark and noisy. Longs was brooding. Any confidence I had left was turning to fear. Walking in the woods by moonlight, I found I remembered with great accuracy every scary movie I had ever seen and every campfire story I had ever heard. The wind howled, seeming to mimic a screech, scream or growl. I was jumpy, constantly scanning the woods with my dim headlamp. I was all but positive I saw a bear on more than one occasion. Of course it was an old tree stump, but that didn't stop adrenaline from flooding my veins.

Walking into the face of fear requires faith sprinkled with a bit of stupidity. Whenever anyone takes a risk, you'll usually find thumbprints of these two attributes. Perseverance in the face of an obstacle was something we had both learned in life, and it translated well into mountain climbing.

We reached timberline and emerged from the forest just as the sun's glowing bulb peaked over the crest of the mountain to the east. I had only seen a sunrise once or twice before, but never like this. We stood firm in the wind and watched the darkness scatter across the land. This was a triumphant moment for me. We had made it through the night walking uphill into the wind. That day the wind had become a force that demanded respect.

When you can stand your ground in the face of adversity, something is forged deep within—that is, until a strong gust of wind knocks you over. Dad had barely uttered his words, "Beautiful, isn't it?" when I was suddenly flat on my butt. I smiled. "Yeah, it's beautiful . . ." Two beautiful happenings: the sun rising and me falling down.

The fierceness of the wind in the trees was nothing compared to what we now faced on the exposed mountainside. I rapidly smeared sunscreen across my wind-burned cheeks and trudged on. On more than one occasion, we were both blown clear off the trail, stumbling into delicate vegetation. In the midst of all my effort, the wind announced my insignificance. All we could do was laugh and keep walking. And so, for a total of six hours, we persevered to finally reach the infamous Boulder Field, an odd stretch of flat ground littered with thousands of giant boulders, many that were the size of small cars.

If you want to climb Longs in two days or traverse the peak

from more technical routes, the Boulder Field is the place to camp. We came across a couple of dirty and bewildered campers huddled together to stay warm.

"How was the night?" I asked. My enthusiasm was clearly offensive to them.

"Oh, just fine," one of them said. "I got up to take a leak, turned around, and my tent was gone. Lost in the madness of this stupid mountain. Four-hundred-dollar tent. I had the largest rock I could carry on it. This shit is crazy."

The journey continued. On the other side of the Boulder Field is a landmark called the "Keyhole." The Keyhole is a small ledge you cross to traverse the back side of the mountain. The route gets much more technical past this point, requiring rock scrambling and passing through the dreaded Trough. The summit is not far from the Keyhole in terms of mileage; as far as time and energy go, however, it is considered the halfway mark.

Rumors from other hikers told of worse wind past the Keyhole. Exhaustion was starting to set in. The thought of doing anything remotely technical in this windstorm was insanity beyond me. When I thought of crawling through the Trough in the wind, my ego deflated. Being anywhere near a steep ledge in this kind of wind was terrifying.

Before officially giving up, however, we decided to see what was on the other side of the Keyhole. We climbed the large rocks to an old stone shelter. On hands and knees we peered over the ledge. The wind slapped my burned cheeks. My ears rung. I couldn't breathe. It was impossible to keep my eyes open. There was no conceivable way I could stand, let alone scramble on the rocks.

"Dad, I'll race you to the summit!" I yelled with sarcasm and a sliver of optimism. Maybe he saw a solution that I didn't.

"Absolutely not! You think I'm crazy?" he yelled back.

"Dad, if there were a million dollars on top and it were mine for the taking, I wouldn't go."

"You bet your life you won't go!" His fatherly instinct to protect was in full bloom.

We scrambled back down to the Boulder Field, nestled in some rocks and ate lunch. Dad did what he always does when he's been taken down a notch.

"Look at us, Nate. We're beaten. We got up at two in the morning and stumbled through grueling wind, only to turn around." He laughed and laughed.

He was having fun with this. *Is he mocking me?* I thought. This was not funny! This was serious. Everest was calling my name. I had to be a great mountain climber.

"Great fun, isn't it!" he stated, looking at me with childlike innocence and waiting for my affirmation.

And there it was! The birth of an appetite that would change my life. I had fought alongside my father in another battle, and in his innocent laughter I saw a unique strength that I wanted. He didn't need this experience to define him. It didn't matter what happened. He just wanted to be with me. He was over himself and had no delusion about who he was.

He had nothing to prove!

I didn't have to be bound to achieving.

And so with a bit of unsettling reluctance, I laughed my illusions of mountain prowess away. Stumbling through the mighty wind, I had found my place.

7

A MUCH-LOVED NOTHING

CREATED SOULS HAVE BEEN SCRAPING out life on earth for thousands of years. The world is currently comprised of 6.7 billion inhabitants. The amount of people who have come and gone is beyond my comprehension. I am utterly lost in understanding the mystery of God's pursuing love for eternal dust. I am equally haunted by the insanity of God's relentless unconditional love for *me*—a speck of sand on the beach of humanity.

I am also a grateful speck. Millions have been slaughtered around the world just within my lifetime. There's no reason to think that millions more won't be massacred before I die. Of the billions who have made this spinning sphere their temporary quarters, most have directly seen the blood of war and felt the pain of hunger. I have not. War, famine, diseases, natural disaster, genocide and other evils have systematically deprived countless masses the opportunity to know a father or mother or to watch sons and daughters grow into adulthood. In the whole of human existence, I am extremely fortunate to even know my father, let alone have the opportunity and physical luxury to climb beautiful mountains. The tragic reality for so many only serves to highlight my insignificance and gratitude. Realizing my place in the context of humanity and internalizing my irrelevance are wonderful remedies for my pride.

The implications of being loved just as I am are staggering. It was becoming clear that if I really understood that I was loved by God, I would have no need for pride or the crushing desire for others' approval. Knowing I was loved was liberation from myself and from my silly ambitions. I was becoming a little child, free to explore the world with zero to prove.

◆　◆　◆

With the newfound freedom Longs offered, I set my sights on Mount Massive. This was also the perfect time for my older brother who lived in Kansas to join in on our excursion. Joel could not understand why we wanted to hike for twelve hours up a steep incline in the blistering sun, intense wind and dangerous lightning. For Joel, the idea of doing something potentially dangerous and painful is idiotic at best. In the end, I think he wanted to spend time with Dad and me. So I abused his charity by talking him into something he had no interest in doing.

I was eager to outfit Joel in my old, mismatched, cheap gear. He looked silly and he knew it. I, on the hand, sported a fresh array of mountaineering attire. Nonchalantly I modeled my adventure wardrobe: synthetic fiber pants that converted into shorts, moisture-wicking rain gear with custom armpit zippers and a name-brand backpack complete with lumbar support. To top it off, I flaunted a pair of French Gore-Tex boots, handcrafted for alp adventures. I was a proud mountain man, far removed from my Midwestern roots. I even had my own Sherpa, a seventy-five-pound German Shepherd–husky mix that looked surprisingly similar to a wolf.

Owning a dog is the staple of all self-respecting, twentysomething Coloradans. Ever since I was a child, I longed to have a furry companion; Ziggy was mine. He was as loving and adventurous as I had ever hoped to be. I felt like a proud parent standing next to Ziggy, who was all decked out in his thickly padded waterproof pack stuffed with his water and my lunch. I had equipped my dog better for this journey than my own brother.

Growing up, I was the challenged child. In grade school my brother was tested for being gifted; I was tested for learning disabilities. As a kid, Joel spoke Spanish and played the violin in the adult city orchestra; I did lots of drugs. My brother tried to be a good son and make my parents proud; I grew my hair long and drew anarchy signs on my clothes with a Sharpie.

My brother does exceptionally well at every endeavor that he attempts. In fact, he is such a gifted person that I rarely tried to compete. There was really no use, since I always fell short. For a brief moment though, I thought this just might be my chance to excel at something. Joel lived at sea level and was sure to puke from the altitude before the day was over. I had seven peaks under my belt and a new set of smoke-free lungs. I guess my pride needed another beating.

Dad and I explained the lessons we had learned about pacing and cautioned Joel of the grueling pain he would experience. As we began the journey at the cusp of dawn, it was clear Joel was not into slowing down. I guess not everyone has to pace themselves. I quickly relinquished all notions of competition and opted to find a slow pace with Dad. Longs continued to teach. It was painful, however, watching Joel's silhouette shrink as he scurried up the mountain, leaving us behind. I didn't even attempt to keep up with him. I don't believe I could have anyway. It was best not to compare myself with my brother. Not only would I fail, but honestly: did it really matter? I smiled and reveled in my newly formed freedom and playfully muttered Longs' echo, "My accomplishments don't define me. After all, I'm just a speck of sand."

As it turned out, Joel had secretly concluded that our guidebooks were written for old, out-of-shape people. And maybe they were. The books listed Massive as twelve hours round-trip. Joel was shooting for six. It would take Dad and me a good fourteen.

As Dad and I crested the summit, Joel looked confused and worried. "What happened? Dad, are you okay?" he asked, in an innocent but slightly cutting tone.

Dad bowed his chest and with gusto gruffed, "I'm great! What? You think you can outdo this old man? Proud little spring chicken! I'll take you!" Dad couldn't manage to keep up the charade and burst into laughter. "This is hard work," he whimpered.

"Are you sure you should be doing this? I mean, at this rate it will be dark before we're done," Joel said, with a hint of sincerity. He was partly right: Dad and I were tired. But the worst was yet to come.

The summit was stunning. There wasn't a cloud in the sky; you could see clear across the state. In the fifteen minutes we stood on the summit, Dad and I identified all the other mountains we had summited. I found myself surprised that my once harsh pride had become soft and gentle.

Joel had time to intensely study the map while he waited. Actually, he probably had time to read half a book. He had determined we could get down faster if we traversed the backside of the mountain and connected with a service road that would lead back to our campsite. This involved descending two thousand feet of scree. Scree is a bunch of small, loose rock fragments, and in this case it rested on an almost vertical pitch. Just stepping on the surface would cause you to slide down the mountain. Ziggy had a low center of gravity and was extremely agile, so he was fine. I found it was best to walk fast, in a skipping fashion. Leaning back against the mountain, I would jump and slide for a good twenty feet. The only problem with this method is that before you stopped sliding you would have to jump again; otherwise your momentum would jerk you headfirst to the ground. It was great fun, but nerve-wracking. Dad found it best to slide on his butt. Joel stayed with him, afraid our father was going to die on the side of this ominous peak.

Ziggy and I cleared the scree field in no time at all. It was my turn to wait, and I welcomed the break. At the southwestern base of the mountain, I discovered a rocky meadow with a wide roaring stream. Absolutely content, I took a nap against a giant boulder. So far I had been unable to teach Ziggy the fine art of pacing, so he had run up and down the trail as we hiked, climbing the mountain at least two times; yet he still had energy to scamper through the flowers and bathe in the stream. I awoke to Dad pouring rocks from his boots. He was clearly exhausted.

❖　❖　❖

Your perineum is a sensitive patch of skin between your genitals and anus. Some believe the perineum is our chamber of light, the portal through which Ka energy enters your body. I believe mine was rubbed raw. Marathon runners smear Vaseline on their perineum and inner thighs to avoid chaffing. It would be years before I learned of this practice. I had been hiking for roughly ten hours and had drunk an excessive amount of water. Before the day was out, my liquid consumption would exceed 300 ounces of water, enough to kill a small child. My excessive sweat, combined with the irritation of ten thousand steps, had created a rash. After my nap, each step brought with it a sharp, chafing pain in my shorts. The more I walked, the more it hurt. We had a good five miles left. I was frightened.

Dad was now hiking slower than his uphill pace on this gentle, descending ground. He was even hobbling back and forth, moving at about the speed of a toddler. His spectator injury was bothering him, and his legs were collapsing from strain. I wondered if his perineum was sore, but I didn't ask. It's not right for a son to ask about the status of his father's perineum.

Through excruciating pain, we finally rounded the mountain and were a half mile to the four-wheel-drive service road. We had now passed the twelve-hour mark, and Joel was anxious to be done. With much gratitude, my dad and I accepted his offer to hike ahead and bring the truck back. The last half mile walking on level ground was the most difficult hiking I had ever done. Upon reaching the makeshift road, I collapsed. Like a slow-motion knock-out punch, my sweat scattered across the dusty earth. I was convinced my fancy shorts would bear a blood stain from my throbbing perineum, but I was too tired to look. Dad moaned dramatically in the distance. He was hurting. Ziggy, the great mountain dog, lay next to me and licked his bloody and cracked paws.

"Look at us, Nate!" Dad panted. "Your brother lives at sea level, and he went to rescue us poor souls. I overdid it. I don't think I can walk another step."

An hour later, my superman brother picked us up. If Longs had spared any of my delusions of mountain expertise, they were now gone. My perineum and I were looking for a hot bath and a cold brew. Joel never puked. He probably arose early the next morning for a brief jog. I slept for twelve hours straight.

I would not rise from this experience to fight another battle in the same way. The memory of this defeat would squelch my pride. Instead of retreating to the old lies about myself, however, I opted to let the ideas I learned on Longs sink deep into my consciousness.

My accomplishments didn't matter.

Failure didn't define or diminish me.

I could just be.

I was a nothing.

I was a much-loved nothing.

This was liberating.

8

HUMILITY IS FOR LOSERS

I HONESTLY EXPECT ACCOMPLISHED PEOPLE to be arrogant. Pride is so much a part of our culture that I seldom identify it as anything odd. From sporting events to movies, pride is a celebrated virtue. Children are indoctrinated into thinking that they live in the best society the face of the earth has ever seen. It's called "patriotism," but I think "conceit" might be a better word.

With Christ's clear call to be last, you would think Christians might be different. Yet when we erect statues and name buildings after ourselves, it is evident that we're not immune from the collective sin of pride. Is it because we're so obsessed with being number one that even our churches bear the distinction of "First" by name? We don't expect humility from our leaders when they rise to the top. We reserve humility for losers.

❖   ❖   ❖

Mountains were proving large enough to put my pride in its proper place. But I didn't want the summer to end with our thrashing on Massive. My remaining arrogance required that we go out on top, so we opted for a doubleheader: Grays and Torreys Peaks.

Our trusty guidebooks stated that it was possible to climb both peaks in one day. The task would require only an extra two thousand feet of elevation: one thousand down a saddle, and one thousand up the remaining peak. The base of the mountain was high enough to begin with, so that summiting both peaks would require much less effort than our other adventures. As I expected, Dad was skeptical that such a feat was possible, particularly since our last two fourteeners had bordered on disaster.

We arrived the night before and camped in a stunning forest at the eastern base of the mountains. A jagged rock wall cradled the two sister peaks in a bowl-like fashion. The face of the wall was arranged with layer upon layer of diverse sediment. Our ascent began just as the sun peered over the stunning rock bowl. The cracks and crevices bore long shadows, revealing an array of colors.

We spent most of the first hour on the trail marveling at the rock wall. The sun's delicate dance smattered the wall in orange, yellow, purple and red. It seemed as if every moment a new color would appear and an old one fade. We spoke few words and took many pictures.

It was Saturday and about as crowded as a fourteener gets. Dad and I found our enduring pace: dreadfully slow but steady. Countless other hikers passed us by. Dad greeted virtually every one. "You just go right on ahead. We'll see you on your way down. I'm the slow one. My son is nice enough to wait for me," he would state, trying to save my pride. I smiled, content to crawl up the trail—at least until Sequoia Boy and his pungent cologne blew past us.

"Sequoia Boy" was my name for a fortyish, middle-management-looking fellow with chiseled calves that reflected the giant tree. He was as serious as I had recently hoped to be, complete with the irritated look of a man on a mission. He ignored Dad's greeting and gruffly shouted back at his traveling companion, who was still some fifty feet down the trail.

"Hurry up, Jeff, or I'm going to leave you like I did yesterday on Longs. We're thirty minutes behind schedule! We *will* knock out Pikes Peak in the morning before we fly back to L.A." He was clearly putting on a show for us.

Dad casually smiled. "You know, Nate, our slow pace serves to make others feel good about their abilities."

"Dad, they're doing four peaks in three days," I whispered, clearly intimidated.

"Why?" he asked. "That doesn't sound like fun to me."

I glanced at the changing rock bowl again; it was now a pale gray with a hint of yellow. He was right. This was supposed to be enjoyable. I smiled. It felt good to be myself—to be a loser, comparatively speaking. In fact, I couldn't believe I had wanted to be like that guy. He probably missed the rock bowl, and he certainly missed the flowers. I reveled in my nothingness and marched on. It was a joy to take my place at the end of the line. Sequoia Boy could have his glory around the water cooler on Monday; I didn't need it.

We slowly hiked our way through a series of switchbacks toward the summit of Grays. When we arrived, we found that the summit was dotted with people talking and chatting as if it were some sort of mountaineering reunion.

You depend on other hikers for help if a need should arise. This often forms camaraderie on fourteeners. Too bad I'm not aware of my need for others off the mountain. Usually my dad and I would avoid conversation with other hikers, but today it was inevitable. Dad must have been taken by the communal experience because he was walking around with a goofy smile, eager to chat. When I heard a woman asking Dad about his experiences on other fourteeners, I just knew he would draw me in.

"Oh, I don't do much. My son—now he's the real mountain climber," Dad told her enthusiastically, motioning in my direction.

She turned to me with a cheerful, inquiring look. "Have you scaled a lot of peaks?" she asked.

Now: earlier this was the kind of question I had lived for. In my head I had rehearsed the name, location, elevation and various details about every mountain I had climbed. Earlier, my reply would have started with some obligatory humility so as to not look too eager, but then I would have slowly shifted into a few dramatic tales of my experiences that would have trumped hers. Once I had proved my mountaineering worth, she would have been impressed and I would have been reminded of my own value and worth—all because I had done lots of meaningless crap and been able to articulate it with some sort of precision. That was the sort of rubbish I had bought into.

Today I smiled and instead opted for Dad's tone. "Oh, not really," I said. "We've done a few. The mountain usually beats me up pretty good. How about you?"

Before the day was over, for some strange reason, Dad would run this same "My son is a real mountain climber" act with three other people. Each time I would answer in roughly the same manner. What was he doing? Did he know how much these mountain-eering accomplishments had recently meant to me? Was he test-ing me? Providing an opportunity for me to practice my newfound humility? Either way, I smiled at myself and my new growth. I was really starting to like this father-son bit. Actually, looking back, I imagine my father probably gave his words little thought and was just diverting the attention away from himself. I was starting to feel like a better person whenever I was around him. This was a genuine gift.

◆ ◆ ◆

Before we started spending all this time together, I didn't know much about my father's professional life. He didn't talk about it much, and most likely I took little interest in it anyway. I can sum up my previous knowledge of my father's career in eight points.

- I knew that he used to teach at a small school called "Friends University." (When I was a teenager, the school's initials always made me laugh.)

- I knew that his books impressed some lady so much that she bought me a pair of black leather Nike roller skates when I was in grade school. (It was my first pair of name-brand foot apparel.)

- I knew that he started some small organization with a name no one could pronounce because it was in Latin.

- I knew that the obscure name of the organization was purpose-ful so that it would not turn into some commercial enterprise. (This didn't make sense.)

- I knew that he quit a job that gave him three months off a year in order to work full-time at the Latin-named organization, which didn't really pay him because he gave the money back. (Once again, this made no sense.)

- I knew that some guy said he was a freaky New Age guru who might as well have studied with Buddhist monks. (That one sounded cool, but it was so far from reality that it made me laugh. Dad didn't laugh. Mom cried.)

- I knew that my mom picked out nice clothes for him to wear when he spoke because he had no sense of fashion. (I thought anyone who voluntarily wore a suit was insane.)

- I knew that he got to travel all around the world and didn't care about getting to see those places. (Insanity again.)

What I didn't know is *what* people wanted to hear him talk about. I never stopped to ask. Kids are funny like that.

During these hikes I was becoming interested in my father, and I started to research things about him. It was through asking probing questions during our countless hours on the trail that I began to learn about his accomplishments and what it was that he spoke about to crowds.

Most people in the world don't know who my father is, and many who do couldn't care less. Yet in some circles, as I came to find out, he is quite the little celebrity. According to *Christianity Today*, Dad is the only living author to appear in the top ten "Most Significant Christian Books of the 20th Century." I once heard it said that his impact will not be measured in years or decades, but in centuries. All this from a man who misplaces his keys or wallet at least once every time I go anywhere with him. I found it amazing that he could bear such high distinctions and yet manage to have minor collisions while driving every one of my cars (with the exception of my current vehicles and that's because he has never driven them). The guy even smashed up my vintage Airstream travel trailer—not once, but twice. I don't mean to be cruel, but at times he seems to struggle with completing basic tasks, like turning on and off his computer. While he's a little clueless at times, for all intents and purposes he is a most ordinary person.

My father's worldly accomplishments came as a bit of a surprise to me. His humility and shortcomings had thrown me off. Had he spoken boastfully about his work, I might have thought otherwise.

◆　◆　◆

Humility receives scant praise or training in our culture. We live in a breeding ground for egomania. I didn't really understand my father's humility. While I would proudly proclaim to strangers the shallowest of my accomplishments, my father would not. On the trail my father spoke with humility about his climbing. He would say it was out of necessity—it's impossible *not* to be humble when you are struggling as much as we were. Realistically, few people pushing sixty could climb a fourteen-thousand-foot mountain—or want to, for that matter. But his humility clearly extended beyond the mountain. I began to uncover story after story of times that Dad sought to advance others rather than himself. He seemed to take great delight in helping to launch other people's careers while paying very little attention to his own. I began to learn stories of his efforts to help bring others into the public eye. It turns out that my father has had ample opportunity to move toward higher status and fame; with a smile, he has turned it away. It's almost as if he doesn't care about these things. I think years ago he cared more, but now he's certainly content to prove or be nothing. He turns down high-profile speaking opportunities and seeks small substantive gatherings. I guess I should have expected that from a guy who wrote a book on simplicity. Through the years, my dad has continually written about what he felt was important rather than what sells more books. He runs from turning his work into money-making, gift-store gimmicks. His humility has forged a sort of purist, nonconformist notion of the way to handle his affairs. My dad the radical?

I was starting to reckon the man I knew growing up with the person I was beginning to respect. When I was a kid, we weren't necessarily tied in to a community of people, so his public image was not something I had much exposure to. My childhood disappointment in his lack of involvement in my life led me to hate whatever it was he was off doing. His work did hold some perks, however. He usually brought me back matchbooks from his trips to add to my expansive collection, and once a year he would take me on one of his speaking trips. On these trips nice people would give me gifts and take me for a tour of the area while Dad worked. I no longer had an entire wardrobe of secondhand clothes, and when I was ten we got to go to Hawaii. But I was largely disconnected from his job, as I guess most kids are from their parents' work. I didn't grow up holding my father's success in high esteem, and his public persona never seemed real to me. The paradox of his home life and public life is a mystery I am still unpacking.

❖   ❖   ❖

One time when I was a kid, Dad brought home this giant fluorescent sign his publisher was throwing away. Our family assembled in the darkened living room, and my dad plugged in the giant sign, revealing a glowing, three-foot headshot of himself. We laughed for hours. His face was so big, like he was someone important. We were unable to take the luminous bust of my father seriously. Honestly now: you have to admit the marketing tools we are so accustomed to seeing are downright ridiculous.

My mother has been a good source for my father's humility. While her love for him is clear, she is truly unimpressed.

"Carolynn, I know how to sweep the floor," my father moaned.

"You're doing it the wrong way. Do I need to show you again?" Mom playfully hammered. "Thirty years of marriage and you'd think he'd learn. I've had to teach your father how to do just about everything. Not once, not twice, but over and over again. Helpless . . . just helpless," Mom joked. "He goes and speaks, and everyone thinks he's so great. I've got to live with him and he can't even care for himself. Keep him humble: that's what I do! He writes these great books and can't even sweep a floor!"

Maybe Dad stayed humble professionally for the same reason that he stayed humble on the trail: he knew himself. On the trail it was plain to see that we were outmatched. In fact, we were quite possibly the worst hikers on the mountain. Maybe my father has enough awareness of his shortcomings to balance out any illusions of greatness.

I was in the habit of viewing myself at the center of a universe that should bend to my will. Watching my dad view his worldly accomplishments as largely irrelevant was having a profound impact on me.

I was starting to understand that overcoming my bondage to accomplishment gave me not only freedom but also, paradoxically, the motivation to work hard. Could I lovingly embrace my short-comings with a gentle heart, remaining ever aware of my need for God's redemption? I was beginning to wonder if the excessive shaming embedded in Christian culture had only served to re-inforce my self-centered nature. As I began to really understand that I was loved, I found myself enabled to do my best with the few gifts and talents I had. As they say in Alcoholics Anonymous, "Suit up and show up." Who I was becoming and my capacity to love others extravagantly are what mattered. Isn't it impossible to put others first when arrogance rules the day? If the biblical mandate is to be last, then certainly humility is for losers.

◆　◆　◆

From the top of Grays, the journey to Torreys looked like a short venture. After eating our sun-scorched lunch, we pushed on toward Torreys Peak. Down the rocky side we greeted an expansive saddle that separated the two mountains. The uphill march was about to begin.

9

ON FALSE SUMMITS

IN THE EARLY 1900S, EUROPEANS RACED to explore the remaining edges of the earth. The Brit Robert Falcon Scott made multiple dangerous attempts to be the first to set foot on the South Pole. In January of 1911 he finally reached his frozen destination, only to discover that weeks earlier the Norwegians had won. Discouraged, the crew began the nearly two-thousand-mile return trip home. The trek required maintaining a certain pace for survival. On the day before his thirty-second birthday, one of the men, Lawrence Edward Grace Oates, realized he could no longer continue. He had an old war wound and was horribly crippled by frostbite. Rather than risk the lives of his fellow companions, he left his tent and walked into the oblivion of a -20 degree blizzard, stating simply, "I am just going outside and may be some time." Oates had given all he had to make it to the Pole and had saved nothing more for the return trip. The rest of the crew would be dead within weeks, eleven miles from needed provisions.

Sometimes when my boots scratch the earth, I think of past adventurers, and like a young boy I borrow some of the drama. Today, on my way up Torreys, I was staggering along. My muscles had hardened. I had nothing left. I was scraping the edges of my will. After an hour of torment, the end was in sight.

"Look! There's the summit. Dad, we're almost there," I puffed, pointing north to our clearly visible destination.

"Nah, Nate. That's a false summit," he panted confidently.

"*No!*" I screamed.

A mistaken interpretation of what lies ahead as the top of the mountain is a common phenomenon called "the false summit." Thinking that you see the end in sight, only to discover that more agony awaits you, is an awful realization. On a steep pitch, correctly identifying your destination is nearly impossible. This process can play out any number of times on the same mountain and surely motivated many a weary traveler. It's much easier to keep going when you think the end is near.

Dad was right. Much to my dismay, this was to be a false summit. I should know this about life by now. Just when I think I've arrived, I'm almost always mistaken. With a loud grunt, I rallied my aching legs and trudged on.

❖   ❖   ❖

Recently I heard about a friend donating his time to work with a group of young men. For the last two years, he had done his work largely in secret. I told him I had heard about how much the boys appreciated a busy man giving of his time and how seldom adults took an interest in the lives of youth. His response made me queasy: "Oh, it's all God," he said sheepishly, looking at the ground with embarrassment.

"Yes, but you have shown up every week. You've given your free time to others. I just want to encourage you in your service," I persisted.

"Oh, I can't take that. Anything good that comes out of our meetings is a total God thing," he replied.

"I'm not talking about the group's success," I responded, more forcefully than the situation called for. "I'm trying to acknowledge that you're doing something really selfless." My friend was clearly annoyed and abruptly changed the subject.

I knew his line, as I had spewed it many times before myself. It may have looked like humility. His intentions may have been pointed in the right direction, but in the end I was only gazing on humility's false peak. He was only responding to an unspoken pressure from cultural Christianity: putting on a religious show so others will think better of us. This norm is more akin to a prideful lie than humility. The mere fact that I'm breathing right now is a "God thing." It's a given that at this very second, God is maintaining the existence of every living thing. But God is not making my choices. When we make a good choice, this should be celebrated, so as to encourage future decisions and to spur each other on toward love and good works (Hebrews 10:24). How can I spur you on if you won't acknowledge that you played any role in the situation? I potentially discount God's process in me when I fail to accept an appropriate compliment.

Years ago when people complimented my dad, he would look down and mumble something about how he wasn't worthy. My dad's good friend Dallas used to call it "the humble mumble." Dad has since quit. If you compliment him now, he responds with a standard line. Looking you in the eye with a soft confidence, he states, "I'm glad my little work has been helpful to you."

❖　❖　❖

Many things in life I just can't rush, but having an awareness of the growth I need is no reason to shut my eyes. It's painful to realize that I'm not at the place spiritually or interpersonally that I once thought or wished I was. Now, standing on what I previously had thought was the summit, I realized that I had a long way to go toward substantial humility. I was in the habit of denying my personal false summits. Denial is such a useful tool for coping with disappointment in oneself. But on the mountain I couldn't fool myself: I either summited or not.

Once again a slow and steady pace yielded compensation, and we reached the top. Amazingly, no other person was in sight. The mass crowd of the day had gone home. We had been some of the first people on the mountain, and we were quite possibly going to be the last to leave. We were in no hurry. The weather was pristine and our conversation was golden. We sat on top of the mountain and talked about nothing and everything for a good hour. I was tired and content.

During any prolonged physical endeavor, I hit a series of points at which I think I can no longer go on. If I push through, I pass a threshold of sorts, after which the work becomes much easier than before. After following the rhythm of one foot in front of the other, I reached a certain grace, and the descent down Torreys glided by. At the base of the trail we reached a service road and began the final mile to our campsite. The peppy lady I had spoken with earlier drove past, stopped her car and motioned for us to join. Without hesitation, or word, we piled in the backseat.

For the first time since I was a little child, I was starting to be okay with myself. My life was decent. I was getting ready to graduate from college, my wife and I were getting along more than not, and the father-son thing was starting to work out. I was also in the best shape of my life. I was putting away years of self-loathing and learning how to live. I was even starting to flirt with happiness. It almost seemed like I was getting things together. Yet once again, I was peering at a false summit.

10

FREEDOM TO QUESTION

WINTER HAD COME, AND OUR mountain excursions continued. Loveland Ski Resort is cheap, never crowded and devoid of traffic. The ski lift takes you to the top of the Continental Divide with breathtaking wind and views. Tourists prefer the name-brand resorts; locals ride at Loveland.

It was early season, and we were having our pictures taken for our pass cards. We were excited and unorganized; our shoelaces were dangling, and we kept dropping mittens and hats. Dad never seemed to be able to wrangle his ski poles into position and ended up misplacing his wallet and glasses on more than one occasion.

"Nathan Foster," announced an attractive girl from back East, who had probably left home to work at a ski resort and live in a two-bedroom trailer with ten other people. It was picture time! "That's me," I stated, nodding confidently. I had arrived. I was getting a

Loveland card, and I was cool. I sported a smooth grin as the camera flashed, forever immortalizing my status as a Colorado local.

"Richard Foster," she called. "Hey, you two look alike! Are you guys brothers?"

Dad stood on his tiptoes, tilted his head upward and adopted my confident nod. "That's right, ma'am," he exclaimed playfully. "Brothers!"

I smiled. This was a double compliment. Dad didn't feel so old, and I didn't feel so young. *Brothers*, I thought. *That's got a nice ring to it.*

◆　◆　◆

Having a religious author and ordained minister as a father, you might assume that I was raised on a steady diet of Christian indoctrination and spiritual formation. This was not the case. Most of the spiritual talk came from my mother in her "God is really disappointed in you and you need to repent" lecture. She was raised Southern Baptist, and this was standard fare. We went to church Sunday mornings, prayed before meals and bedtime, and Mom encouraged us to read our Bibles. I remember a couple of occasions when Dad tried doing some sort of scriptural reading around the dinner table. It never went over well. The seriousness of his tone made me feel claustrophobic. That was pretty much the extent of it. I'm sure more was said, but that's the bulk of what I heard. I honestly have no recollection of my father ever teaching me or my brother about Christianity. That's not to say such teaching didn't happen; it may well have, but I just don't remember. Actually, I don't remember much about my father growing up. Remember, he was the serious, silent ghost.

To some extent, I'm sad that issues of faith were not more a part of my upbringing. I hate to think the majority of my Christian teaching came from Sunday school. Well-intended as it is, with all of the focus on behavior and obeying your parents, Sunday school can inadvertently become a breeding ground for legalism. Looking back now, I can't help but think that having my dad unpack the Sunday service over lunch could have been a rich part of my childhood. Of course, the developmental window between when a child is able to understand and when he or she stops being willing to listen is pretty short. My preteen aversion to anything spiritual from my dad probably didn't help matters either.

My home did give me the freedom to make my own choices, for which I'm thankful. Families with children devoid of any personality and independent thought freak me out.

◆   ◆   ◆

At age sixteen, I let go of trying to manage my crumbling life and surrendered to Jesus as best I understood him. Without the knowledge of my parents, I began attending a local church. In part, this was a beautiful and magical time. Life felt new. I was sincerely trying to make good decisions. I did my best to accept the church and its norms as authorities not to be questioned. I was an astute student at learning what was expected of me. I shunned my sinful friends by excessive judgmental witnessing, and I frequented the Christian bookstore. I cleaned up my language, vowed I would never touch drugs or alcohol again, and at least once a week attempted to quit smoking and jerking off. I spent my free time listening to Christian music and memorizing key Scriptures for mission trips. I lied about the wonder of my quiet times and determined that when life didn't work out, I must not be trying hard enough for God. I even wore a shirt with Bible verses on it for at least half a day.

Since junior high, I had been in the habit of mistrusting any form of establishment. Now that I was doing the Christian thing, I was desperately trying to put the "Question Authority" mantra behind me. I chalked up my ideas that something was wrong with the church to my sinful nature or possible brain impairment from drug usage and head injuries. I was trying to be the package I thought God and others wanted me to be: a Scripture-quoting, sedated, nonoffensive monk who followed all of the rules.

Even with all my religious fervor, I was horribly embarrassed about letting my parents know that I was trying to give my life to God. It would feel like I was saying that they had been right and I had been wrong. In reality I *was* wrong—just not about every-thing. And they *were* right—just not about everything. I flew out a kite to let my parents know of my newfound religion by putting a Christian fish sticker on my truck. Months later, my mom in-quired why I hadn't removed it. She just assumed the fish had been there when I bought it. I sheepishly corrected her. When I decided to be baptized, I didn't plan to invite my parents. They overheard a conversation, however, and then I felt obligated.

By twenty, when I started all this mountaineering madness with Dad, I had quit trying to look or act like a Christian. I was over the religion thing, yet I was intently interested in Jesus. I would bounce in and out of churches working and volunteering, always trying to find my place, always somewhat disillusioned. I met many wonderful people and had some great experiences, but I was lost in the tension between goodness and disgust. I craved the authentic expressions of life I had found in the world, but the love of God continued to stalk me. I was irresistibly drawn to and confused by the light of Jesus. My prayer life was tearful and intimate. With a searching posture, I navigated prolonged isolation and experienced a painful yearning for God. I found myself sinning when I attended church, since my judgment of others there was overwhelming. Socially I was more comfortable with non-Christians. My life was a ragged attempt at discipleship. I was afraid to speak many of my real thoughts on Christianity for fear that I would be discounted as turning my back on God. I was becoming comfortable with the idea that I had adopted the religion of my parents, yet still I didn't really talk with my dad about issues of faith.

Occasionally my father would speak to a local gathering, and I always tried to make it. In one of these talks I heard him say the most alarming thing. "You wouldn't have liked me back then. I was so serious." The crowd laughed. I didn't. Was he really aware of how solemn he had been? Had he made a conscious effort to chill out? I took this as his kite.

◆　◆　◆

The dilapidated chair on the old ski lift creaked, swaying violently as it carried us up to the top of the world. The wind screamed ice pellets that splattered against my goggles. Every inch of my skin was covered, safe and warm amid a sea of down and fleece. Nestled in my giant parka, I exposed my blasphemous thoughts: "I hate going to church. It's nothing against God; I just don't see the point. Why would I want to get up early on my day off only to sit while someone talks at me? Plus, it seems like my only two choices in church are enduring either an irrelevant funeral march or else an entertaining plastic show."

I didn't know how to talk about Christianity with my dad, so negativity seemed like the easiest place to start. Plus, he would surely launch into some lecture, and I could say I had tried. I braced myself for the rebuke. After all, I was criticizing the institution that he had given his professional and personal life to serve.

"Sadly, many churches today are simply organized ways of keeping people from God," replied Dad.

"What?" I laughed. "I can't believe you just said that!"

"Well, it's true." Through the raging wind, his words rang with empathy and sadness. At a minimum I had expected a well-crafted argument; not this. Rather than explore his comment further, I took this as my chance to unleash a well-rehearsed, cynical rant I had been aching to share with someone.

"Okay, so since Jesus paid such great attention to the poor and disenfranchised, why isn't the church the world's epicenter for racial, social and economic justice? I've found more grace and love in the worn-out folks at the local bar than those in the pew. And then we base our institutional success, and consequently declare God's blessing, by the number of new converts and by the attendance on Sunday morning. It's like we're some dehumanizing womanizer keeping tallies on our bedpost. Discipleship is an afterthought that no one is prepared to actually do. Jesus' example of investing time in a few people for a number of years has no room in the mix of building projects, attracting new members and balancing budgets. And instead of allowing our pastors to be real humans with real problems, we prefer some sort of overworked rock stars."

Dad smiled. "Good questions, Nate. Overworked rock stars:

that's funny. You've obviously put some thought into this." My rant didn't faze him in the slightest; if anything, he seemed to find it entertaining. He didn't blow me off or put me down. Where was the overly serious man? This was weird.

As we approached our destination, the lift chair abruptly stopped. Protected from the elements by a ravine, we swayed in the air and Dad offered a new idea. "What people so desperately need today is space, stillness and attentiveness," he said. "And what so many churches major in are busyness, hurry and noise. We keep people constantly distracted. Earnest folks who are searching for a deep, intimate life with God end up being put on some church committee! If, instead, we carefully taught people how to create space in their lives and how to listen attentively, we would then incline their hearts toward God. As it is, we often do almost everything and anything but that."

"Wow, nice thoughts," I replied. "I'm going to chew on that for awhile. Want to spend the night up here?" (I have found odd questions to be useful in rocky verbal transitions.)

"Absolutely not!" exclaimed Dad. "This weather is crazy!"

"I would," I said.

"I'm sure you would. You know you're nuts, don't you? Let's get down from here. This weather gives me the willies." Our conversation was cut short by the end of our ride. We slid off the chair and down the icy ramp.

I love extreme weather and the tension it brings: the fright, intensity, beauty and exhilaration. Through the bitter cold, we rode down the mountain. I shivered with gladness: I had done it. I had broached the subject of faith. Well, sort of. Either way, Dad's words and validation were extremely important. Sometimes it's the crushing of fearful expectations that ushers in change.

This was the first of many conversations about faith and the church that Dad and I had. Lift-chair discussions continued all winter long. Whether he intended to or not, my father gave me permission to seriously listen to some of the thoughts and ideas in my own head. I was allowing myself to ask questions, and it felt good. I was also discovering a certain grace in talking with my dad. He turned out to be a wonderful listener who asked thoughtful questions. My father never put me down or treated me as if I were stupid. He usually only offered advice when I prodded, and he was extremely respectful and encouraging of my journey. The overly serious religious icon had dissipated when I wasn't looking. I began to look forward to conversations and casually planned topics to cover.

That winter a shift began. I was learning that a balanced critique is not bad, but that it is actually a positive and healthy part of engaging our society. Only when we care about something do we take the time to give it a critical look. Acknowledging where we fall short is necessary in order to do better. It is only individuals and social structures addicted to power and control, such as abusive and demagogic cult leaders, that can't handle critique. Once I allowed myself the freedom to ask questions, I no longer felt like a cynic dissing God but rather like a powerless man with a deeply broken heart. My ideas were coming out of a place of investment. If I wasn't captivated by the Jesus life, I would have been done with the whole charade years ago.

By the end of winter, my questions began transforming into ideas for action. Somewhere amid the wind and snow of the Continental Divide, I decided that if I'm not willing to be an agent of change, my critique is a waste. It's an easily overdone cliché to rip on the American Christian church. But am I willing to weep for what she could be? Am I willing to work for change even if it is small and seems insignificant? Some days I am. Most I'm not.

Ideas that needed years to simmer had found their way to me. I now felt the freedom to question. I began redefining what I had called "church" into the New Testament concept of the body of Christ. When we're in the midst of other believers, do we make up the church? What did, or could, this look like? Regardless of how it's defined, I was learning that the church was simply a collection of broken people recklessly loved by God. Christ suffers for these people; the least I can do is try to love them. Jesus told us he came for the sick, not the healthy, and certainly our churches are a reflection of this truth. I just wish we knew how sick we are. It's the arrogant, judgmental attitude that I find nearly impossible to love. The smooth, seeker-friendly, corporate machines that seem to be replacing the dying denominations aren't much of an improvement. What if we were known for our love? What does it look like when honest, broken human beings get together because they need God and each other?

11

HOW DO YOU
CELEBRATE DISCIPLINE?

IN MY JUNIOR YEAR OF HIGH SCHOOL, my teachers recommended that I learn a trade because I had little hope of continuing my education. Rather than attending normal classes, I spent half of each day learning carpentry at a vocational school. That year I went ahead and got my G.E.D. No one had any expectation that I would ever go to college.

"Today I summit the largest mountain. Today I graduate!" read the invitation. I had done it. And I wasn't nearly as smart or stuck-up as I had imagined a college grad to be. Climbing mountains was much easier than academic work. If it wasn't for the assistance of my brilliant wife, there's no way I could have finished. (I offered to frame half of my diploma for her, but she declined.)

Dad had been my role model as a challenged student. In college he would stand on his head to keep awake as he studied through the night. (I never had *that* type of fortitude.) Perseverance and a willingness to remain teachable kept my father from facing any significant consequences from his academic impairments. Dad was determined to learn, even as an adult.

And so a man of average intelligence, with no real means, plagued with horrible spelling and grammatical skills, became an author.

◆ ◆ ◆

After the summer sun had set, the moon illuminated the stage of the child athlete. The wind transformed small trees into shadowy spectators waving with applause. A worn basketball exposing its woven core was my trophy, marking another season of school-less days and late bedtimes. When I was ten, I could have shot baskets all night. Occasionally Dad would join my brother and me on the magical court. Following the cadence of his pounding palms against the orange orb, his announcer voice would begin: "The disciplined person does what needs to be done when it needs to be done. Now I can take a basketball and put it in a hoop." Then he would unleash a wild shot that would hit high on the backboard and bounce into the grass. Comically shrugging his shoulders, my dad would continue with diminished enthusiasm: "But I can't do it when it needs to be done." I'd laugh so hard I'd nearly pee.

Dad's monologue was his catch phrase: *The disciplined person does what needs to be done when it needs to be done.* My entire family had it memorized, and we always repeated it in a deep and sarcastic tone. Funny how you can memorize something and have no idea what it means. Of course, the bit about his basketball ability was true too. I remember a lot of dramatic grunting. Even today I can picture him darting wildly toward the hoop, often falling over, seldom making a basket.

My dad was the Discipline Guru. I found the title of his first book to be a confusing combination of words: *Celebration of Discipline*. The questions are obvious: Just how do you celebrate discipline? Is this a book about throwing a party whenever you spank your child? Or maybe the book was a collection of narratives about the sadistic joys of self-harm. His book was about neither.

The discipline book was now twenty years old. Dad's publisher was planning a recognition party at George Fox College in Newberg, Oregon. Everyone mentioned in the original acknowledgments would be flown to the gathering. For his line, "My children, Joel and Nathan, were incredibly patient in allowing their daddy to cut short games and stories more than once," I earned a plane ticket and a fancy meal in my favorite state, Oregon. It was time for me to finally read the discipline book.

I secretly became an astute student of my father's professional work. Dad's scripted phrase about shooting baskets encompassed the essence of the book. It really had nothing to do with basketball, and it wasn't nearly as complicated as I previously had thought. What I discovered from his writings were things I already knew intuitively but had been unable to articulate.

Dad's work was based on the premise that if I practiced something, I would get better at it. If I spend years practicing, then when the moment called for my skill, I would be able to respond appropriately. My dad couldn't make a basket when he wanted to because he hadn't spent enough time practicing. His work seemed to uncover a natural process for living. By practicing the spiritual disciplines—things like prayer, meditation and confession—I was training for living as Jesus lived, and hopefully learning to respond to life more like Jesus would if he were to live my life. Dad's book was essentially a how-to manual for practicing twelve of these disciplines.

This was just what I needed to overcome my disillusionment with the religious process. I had all but given up on trying to live a "spiritual life." And faking it was no longer an option. Dad's book engaged me and left me wanting to go and practice weird things like fasting.

❖   ❖   ❖

The recognition of my dad's work in Oregon turned out to be informative and inspiring. I had been largely unaware of the impact of my father's writing, and I discovered many people sincerely affected by his work. Once again I witnessed tears as I heard people speak about the simple book he wrote. Amazing.

Apparently he was the first in modern times to write about the collective spiritual disciplines. Christian denominations are often trained in one or two disciplines but remain unschooled in or unaware of others. By studying various Christian historic movements and the writings of old saints, my dad was able to offer a holistic view of Christendom and the many treasures for spiritual growth she holds. "Bringing the Church to the church" was the original motto of Renovaré, the organization he founded.

Most shocking was to read what authors I greatly admired wrote about my dad. In his endorsement of *Celebration of Discipline*, Ron J. Sider, the evangelical champion of the poor, said that no other book apart from the Bible had been as helpful in nurturing his inward journey of prayer and spiritual growth. Eugene Peterson, translator of *The Message* (which was the main translation of the Bible I would read for the next ten years), remarked once that my dad "found" the spiritual disciplines that the modern world had stored away and forgotten.

I was proud. Even so, questions remained. When I was steeped in legalism, why hadn't my father helped to direct me? Why hadn't he guided me in my journey of faith? Had I really succeeded at hiding my faith from him? Had I closed him off that much? Yet his writing was affecting me like it had so many others.

A few weeks after the trip to Oregon, I received a copy of the twentieth-anniversary edition of *Celebration of Discipline* in the mail. It was blue. The inscription read:

February 1998

To Nathan,
　Wonderful son,
　now affirming friend.
　I love you.
Richard J. Foster
Dad

12

LIVING IN THE MOMENT ON LONGS PEAK

WHERE DID I GET THE IDEA that I deserve to be happy? It's been a brutal process to discover that marriage can sometimes feel like a nightmare, and that work is often tolerable at best.

The other day I heard the ridiculous idea that the film *The Little Mermaid* is full of phallic symbols and that this is indicative of Disney's plot to corrupt our children. What about the *real* damage fairy tales cause? Namely, they perpetuate the lie that if I find the right person, or things, I will live happily ever after. Isn't entitlement to happiness the core presumption of all our media outlets? Or does the lie come from each year being subjected to four hundred billion dollars worth of advertising committed to creating and satisfying my desires? Maybe it comes from childhood, when we chased one entertaining and fun thing after another. Deep down, I believe I deserve to be happy, and I assume that the usual gods—job, money, house, kids and experiences—will deliver. Process is only a means to the end.

◆　◆　◆

Life seemed to be working. I was finding a certain rhythm both on and off the trail. After completing an extended internship at a church, where I worked with addicts on the streets and in the jails, I found the perfect job working in the mountains with high-risk teens in a residential treatment facility. Most of my clients were kicked out of other programs and had served time in jail. They were belligerent, violent and wounded. It was hands-on ministry. One minute a kid would be throwing punches, and the next he'd be sobbing in my arms asking for prayer. Part of my job was to take the boys rock climbing, hiking and backpacking. I even led a few trips up fourteeners. Helping others to summit proved more rewarding than summiting myself. The work was intense. I was happy and exhausted. I was in a zone. It seemed as if only good things lay ahead.

I still stared daily at Longs Peak. Rather than hailing curses at her base, I found myself appreciating contours, snow patterns and the weather she controlled. My anger was shifting to respect. I was beginning to love her. I was ready for another visit. Dad was not.

So I invited a couple of friends from college to meet at the base of Longs and join in the excursion. The wind had colored everything last time, and now the trail looked completely different. I never felt stronger than I did that day on Longs. I found my pace and it was fast. The potential of the human body is amazing. In prayerful meditation I glided up the mountain, reaching the Keyhole in record time.

Huddled in the shadow of a colossal boulder, I soaked my swollen feet in a small stream that melodically gurgled beside me. Occasionally a gust of wind overcame the stream and mist would take flight, sprinkling my head. I was a king. Waiting for my friends, I spent two hours observing the Keyhole and the travelers who crossed her threshold. Most returned, forsaking the summit. Upon reaching my perch, I queried each hiker. "Wind and ice" was the verdict. I had reached my end, again. But I was happy; everything felt right. It was a Louis Armstrong "What a Wonderful World" moment.

◆　◆　◆

Whenever Dad and I were together, it always had an expressed purpose, usually one revolving around some activity or accomplishment. We weren't together just for the sake of being together until our seventeen-day trip to England the month prior to my second attempt at Longs.

Dad was speaking at two huge, weeklong events across England. It was like summer camp for families. In Minehead and Skegness, at semi-run-down vacation resorts on the coast, some forty-five thousand people spent their holiday. Seeing adults run around throwing water balloons at two in the morning was a sight. Dad spoke in a big circus tent. Between camps Dad and I had time to do some sightseeing, so we visited ruins and old churches. We were goofy tourists together, complete with cameras and fanny packs. We stayed at old bed-and-breakfasts, crossing the entire country by train and back again by car. It was great.

By the time we reached the second event, the noisy crowds and British fast food had become too much for us. It was a home-cooked meal that lured us to the chalet of the Northumbria Community. We were welcomed as family by a collection of artists, musicians and unassumingly warm people. They were a dispersed community steeped in the liturgical Christian Celtic tradition. I had no idea you could practice liturgy without the smells, bells and hierarchy of high church. The ancient was new and fresh.

One evening I was invited to join three performers on stage in an interpretive dance set to liturgy. Completely unable to dance, but always open to new experiences, I agreed. After ten minutes of instruction, it was time to present to a packed crowd. My performance was horrible! No one cared. The next evening I was to enter the stage with a flag on a cue from one of the performers. Their accents were thick, which caused me to miss my signal, disrupting the entire song. Again, no one seemed to care.

Late into the night Dad and I joined the community in their tiny chalet for laughter and the evening office (devotions). Dad felt comfortable with these people because no one asked him questions about his work. They were generally unimpressed with him, except when he told a funny joke. What I found in these people were lives centered on building up and cultivating relationships, all for the sole purpose of facilitating community. I am both cynical and perceptive; within a few minutes of meeting people, I can usually ascertain their motives for interacting with me. These people were bent on encouraging one another in Christ's love. A more genuine, graceful and joyful collection of people I had yet to see. They actually seemed content in each moment. The church was being redeemed in my eyes.

❖ ❖ ❖

Nestled in my fortress on the Boulder Field, I had much to think about concerning happiness and living in the present. I concluded that a summit up Longs was not an option that day. I did, however, intend to see the conditions past the Keyhole for myself. My friends finally arrived. They collapsed and began cursing the mountain. I was now free to continue. My heart raced as I pranced from boulder to boulder.

I find few events in adulthood that mimic the intensity, passion and horror of grade school: being called to complete a problem at the chalkboard, or the last day of school for the year. This moment was like those two combined. For five minutes I stood frozen, surveying the rocky climb beyond the Keyhole. "I might be able to do this," I whispered. Yes, the wind was strong, but I'd been in worse. Yes, there was ice, but it seemed to be confined to the cracks and ground. There just might be enough exposed rock to safely scale the mountain. Like a child on the high dive, I motioned my intent to my friends and disappeared through the legendary Keyhole.

Scaling the west face proved workable, other than the sudden burst of wind that threatened to send me down into the rocky abyss. Yet my greater fear came from the realization that I was all alone. If I fell, I could die before anyone would find me.

Examining the mountainside, I spotted two shadowy figures some three hundred feet away. "Where did they come from?" I whispered. Appalachian Trail lore tells of a special phenomenon known as "Trail Angels": mysterious people who appear when you are in need and are never heard from again. Ed and Robert were mine that day. Ed knew the trail and was fearless. He seemed to know how to navigate the ice. Robert, on the other hand, was terrified. Robert's fear was actually a great comfort to me; if he was scared, then I didn't have to be. I would only go on as long as it felt safe. Numerous times I decided to turn around upon reaching a landmark ahead, only to find the continued journey doable. With fear and anticipation, I climbed in God's presence. I was fully awake to each step. Not sure whether I would reach the summit, I stopped thinking about the experience as a whole and reveled in each step. In the midst of my discomfort, I found the strangest thing: joy.

"How is it ahead?" I asked a wide-eyed man who was on his way down the mountain. In a thick southern accent he bellowed, "Well, I'll tell ya, I thought this right here was bad, but up ahead was just too much. I'm going home to Mama." His last words brought a smile to my face that lasted the rest of the afternoon. The laughter he and I shared in this brief exchange washed out some of the adrenaline that was causing my temples to ache. I continued to carefully scale the icy rocks, unaware of my bleeding hands.

Just as a wall of black clouds began racing toward Ed and Robert and me, a fluffy snow began to fall. The end of the journey came as a surprise, since I was lost in each step. Tearing up, I meandered through a series of large rocks, looking for the silver geology marker that indicated the summit. I kissed the frozen medal and softly turned around to descend before the snow accumulated. The summit was partially anticlimactic, as much of life seems to be. Reaching the goal was only the natural consequence of each step. Process was the destination.

As the hours of descent crushed my bruised and scraped body, my mind wandered. Christy was pregnant. I was happy and scared. The morning sickness that supposedly only lasts the first trimester was turning out to be "all day and all pregnancy sickness." I had learned that the smell of lettuce was so strong and vile that I had to eat it on the porch so that she wouldn't vomit. I was beginning to feel helpless and a little guilty for playing in the mountains while she was at home, puking. Christy was using her hours of nausea as a source of connection to Christ's torment. She was learning to live in the suffering. Christy, Dad and the people of Northumbria lived in each moment. I did not.

❖   ❖   ❖

"I can be God": the Fall of humankind is found in believing this one lie. Trace back every sin you can imagine, and you will find the thumbprints of the most destructive idea that the world has ever seen. I listen closely to the lie when I attempt to micromanage my affairs and anyone risky enough to get close to me. While my daily choices and attitude will greatly affect the quality of my life, I am fundamentally powerless in my pursuit of the great idol: happiness. I desperately try to shield myself and others from pain, heartache and sadness. Yet the lives of Jesus and the saints testify to the fact that loneliness and troubles are hallmarks of the human experience. If I really understood the redemptive power of pain in shaping me to be like Christ, would I run from it? As unpleasant as they are effective, heartache and troubles are the best teachers I have known. Can joy really be found in the process of suffering? What do I miss when I focus on the goal rather than the process?

Nevertheless, I had bought the lie that life should be without pain. I would soon enroll in a master's program, graduate and become a dad. Life would be picturesque, and I would live happily ever after.

13

SOMETIMES THE DRAGONS WIN

THE SUN BURST THROUGH THE CURTAINS of the bedroom. My head throbbed. Tearing the dried blood that crusted my face to the pillow, I sat up. My tongue counted the stitches below my lip. I gritted my broken teeth. Concrete is ruthless.

Staggering outside, I sat down on the porch and lit a cigarette. I put my head in my lap while the afternoon sun scorched my naked back. Baby in hand, Christy announced through the screen door with fear and worn patience, "Your dad is coming. He can take care of you. Quit drinking or I'm leaving."

I had exhausted the goodwill of my caring wife. I felt the gravity of the situation. I knew I should care, but I didn't. The insanity was winning.

With a sick body and a beaten-up heart, I slumped in the passenger seat as Dad navigated the mountain roads. I must have been a child the last time Dad drove me somewhere. My family had determined that I should spend a week with Dad at a rustic cabin in the mountains to dry out from my two-month binge. I was disoriented enough to do what I was told. I did feel a trace of remorse that my bad choices had earned me a week of vacation, but I needed the rest. Cheek pressed against the window, I eagerly eyed Big Thompson Canyon. I was scared. It was mid-afternoon and the cravings were well on their way. Yet I felt mildly safe knowing that Dad was going to be with me. Isolation would have left me vulnerable to manipulating myself into another drink. I expected anger and disappointment from my dad. What I got was quiet compassion resolute on action. Aren't dads supposed to be mad when their sons neglect their families for drugs and alcohol?

Staring at the road ahead, Dad softly spoke. "Nate, do you want to tell me what happened?"

"Sure, but I don't exactly know. I can't seem to think straight. I feel like I can't breathe."

"Do you need to see a doctor?"

"No. No. I'm fine. I'm not sure if I'm going to sleep or explode."

"I'd prefer you sleep. Get some rest, kid."

❖ ❖ ❖

The concrete showed two significant splatters of blood some twenty feet apart, indicating that I had hit my head at least twice. No one knew how long I had lain unconscious in the driveway. The CAT scan in the emergency room revealed that everything was intact, but for now my cognitive ability seemed severely impaired. Not much was said those first few days. I sat in silence, assuming I had done mental damage beyond repair.

Now, at the cabin, rest and mountain air were proving to be good medicine. The fog was beginning to lift. Resting on a picnic table, chain smoking and sipping Dr Pepper, I began to talk, and Dad requested my story. His concerned, but kind, posture gave me the freedom to let him in. Staring at my bare feet massaging the brown earth, I searched for answers.

"I've struggled with drinking off and on for years. It was always the same. I'd start casually, a few beers here and there. I would drink like others do. This would last a few days or weeks, and then the cravings for more would grow. It became increasingly difficult to drink in a healthy way, and eventually I'd find myself consuming more than I ever intended to. This would last for weeks. I would spiral down in shame and resolve to quit. I've quit drinking hundreds of times. Sometimes it lasted months, and once for even a year, but usually only for a couple of weeks. Often when I tried to quit, I would be drunk by that evening."

"I knew you drank, but how did I miss this?" asked Dad, with more than a tinge of guilt.

"Because I never told you. I was usually in the process of getting things together. Besides, I always drank alone. No one knew. From the best I could figure, this bout started when I was in grad school writing papers. All day long I would labor on a paper, only to produce a handful of jumbled paragraphs. But throw a few beers into the mix and I was Hemingway, punching out page after page. Inevitably I couldn't stop with a few drinks, and my writing would soon become illegible. Alcohol was the medicine that enabled me to work."

Our talk continued. It felt good to let it out. Internally I shivered with a sense of delight. Secrets hold power. Concealed, they breed like mold.

I was beginning to understand just how my drinking ended up extending beyond the writing. Between school, work and a newborn, I had become incredibly taxed. I felt helpless. Alcohol was my way to regain control and to find rest in the chaos. Ironically, it ended up taking control and bringing more chaos. It started with the reawakening of forgotten emotional ghosts. Pain drowned in alcohol festers and grows. My cure had turned on me with a vengeance. Soon anyone and anything that got in the way of my drinking became the enemy. I was lost. Self-will had run riot.

I vaguely remember thinking something was wrong with repeatedly putting out cigarettes on my arms. The stinging of my flesh was cathartic. Insanity began to take shape. I spent evenings slicing my skin to paint on the walls in blood. I thought it was art. Christy was terrified.

Yet in the midst of my madness, God had been making himself known to me in profound ways. In my drunken prayers, God's presence was ever-captivating. My journal would reveal tears of desperation and longing for God. I couldn't reconcile the fact that I was doing something wrong with the fact that God was showering me with love. I have had a tendency to view life in terms of black and white, good and bad, happy and unhappy. I was finding life to be filled with shades of grey, and God ruled over it all. I was starting to come to terms with the fact that I didn't have all the answers.

❖ ❖ ❖

The next afternoon we took a drive up to the classic Rocky Mountain Park destination, Trail Ridge Road. In the shadow of

Longs, the windy road climbs over the Continental Divide, as scary as it is scenic. I had been up this road many times, but that day it felt as if I had never been there before. Peering into the distance, I saw a hidden mystery that gave me hope. The mountains were frightening. I felt humble and a bit brave. The power of God hovered about. I felt stilled by its strength and serenity.

The apex of the Trail Ridge Road is a visitors' center surrounded by small hikes and overlooks. Dad bought me a hooded sweatshirt with a picture of Longs Peak on it, the robe of the prodigal son. It would become my uniform for the next three years. Why was he being so nice? His hours of listening were healing. He didn't bring talent or theological insight; he brought grace. Dad was my hero, although not the type of hero the world would expect. He didn't swoop in or rescue me or fix anything. By simply *being*, he provided a window into the kingdom where guilt was turned upside down and I was able to breathe and hope.

I had spent a number of years running away from my family, fighting desperately to walk on my own. Walking alone in the woods can be dangerous. Walking alone in life is dangerous. I had known for years that I needed people to help guide me. I honestly never thought one of those people would be my dad. He belonged to the world, not to me.

Too weak to hike, I leaned on a rail staring at the sights. Below me stood a twelve-thousand-foot mountain missing half its face. The crumbled mass formed a rocky cove. What looked to be the remains of a once-great glacier covered the inlet. The brown snow was a melting mix of rocks and dirt.

"That snow is dirty," I muttered to Dad.

"Yeah, it is," he replied.

The wind whipped across my face. We sat in silence mesmerized by the scenery. Dad whispered through the howling wind, "In time, new snow will cover the dirt."

"Yeah. Yeah, I guess it will."

14

ACCEPTING THINGS I
CANNOT CHANGE

THE PORCELAIN WAS COOL AND SOOTHING. I hugged it gently, trying to be as quiet as possible. Vomit is noisy business.

"Nathan, are you okay?" Christy's voice was soft and sleepy.

"Yeah, sure, I'm fine. Go back to bed."

"Are you throwing up? Damn! You're drunk, aren't you?"

"No, no. I'm fine . . . just go back to bed. Sorry to wake you."

In the few days since my trip with Dad, I had tried as hard as I could not to drink. The sincere apology I delivered to Christy the previous day wasn't going to count for much now. Good intentions and willpower proved defenseless. I needed something more.

I heard a whimper behind me. There stood my one-and-a-half-year-old daughter, wobbly-kneed and confused.

"It's okay, baby. Go back to sleep."

I spewed again. She began to cry. Christy escorted her out of the bathroom.

"Look what you've done. She deserves better. I won't let you put her through this." Christy knew all too well what a parent's addiction could do to the heart of a child.

Tears stained my face. This was too much. I was plumbing new depths of shame. This was proving to be a bigger problem than any of us had imagined.

Finally, I was humiliated and scared enough to reach out for help. The following months were marked by the hour upon hour that I spent hidden in the corners of smoky twelve-step meetings.

The best way to describe what it is like to stop drinking is to imagine being told you can no longer pee. The first few hours would be uncomfortable, but doable. Even going all day was not too bad as long as I found distractions. After I strung together a few days, however, the fear that my bladder might explode became a reality that consumed my thoughts. Drinking was an obsession that haunted every waking moment. Living became a constant battle. Floating in the back of my mind was the thought that I may never be able to pee again. I did not want to accept any of this. I was told to take it one day at a time. Even so, the night brought insane thoughts. *Maybe I should have just one more drink. Maybe things would be different this time. Maybe I could drink like my fellows. Maybe I could control it.*

And so, for not urinating, I was awarded a series of coins to mark the occasion. I was never without the latest one in my pocket. Silver for one day, red for one month, gold for two, green for three and blue for six. One hundred meetings later, I tightly clinched a bronze medallion marking one year of sobriety. The medallion had cost less than a dollar, but it was worth a million. A small, ragtag group of recovering drunks applauded. We had cake. It was the greatest accomplishment of my life. On such an occasion as this, it was customary to share your experience, strength and hope with the group. My speech went something like this:

"When I first came in here, I heard my story in others'. For the first time in my life I felt connected, like I had found a home. This pissed me off. I didn't want to relate to you. You were a bunch of old drunks."

The room erupted with laughter.

"I thought I was better than all of you." Again they laughed, as I was now telling their story.

"I thought I would learn how not to drink and then be on my way. I had no idea I would learn about how self-centered I really was. Rather than learning how to increase my willpower, I learned to submit my life to the care of God. When you gave me your phone numbers and said I could call anytime, I knew you meant it. I've never seen that kind of care and commitment offered to a stranger. You taught me that serving others sets me free. I did as you suggested. Each night I got on my knees and thanked God for keeping me sober, and each morning I asked how I could be helpful to others. I got my life back. I learned that in order to stay sober, I need you and I need God. Today I am grateful. Thank you."

Other than the people at my meetings and my wife, no one was more involved in my recovery than Dad. He asked the important questions that others shied away from. "How's your sobriety?" "Are you going to meetings? Calling your sponsor?" He always asked these questions with encouragement and optimism, and he never shamed me. It was the type of accountability I needed. On the small milestones Dad sent cards. Six months and he took me out to dinner. As I approached a year, we both concluded it was time for a celebration trip.

I flung my carefully packed backpack into the truck bed and sped down the road. Bronze medallion in hand, I sported a new button-up shirt with a Popeye print reading, "Strong to the finish." I even decided to quit smoking again.

Life had gotten in the way of my dad and me climbing fourteeners. This trip would reclaim what the year had lost. The plan was to pack in fifty pounds of gear to our base camp at eleven thousand feet in the San Isabel National Forest. For the next week we would camp in a lush valley next to scenic Clear Creek. Our base camp would position us within the proximity of three fourteeners. Rumor told of a hidden hot springs in the mountains. This was a dream trip.

The parking lot was heavily wooded. The trail disappeared into the woods at an incline that was usually too steep for trees to grow. With excited and energized hearts, we began our trek.

I have found that the first mile or so of any endurance activity is usually the hardest. Once I work the kinks out of my body and establish my pace, I find a sort of mental zone that propels me up the hill. But my zone was nowhere to be found. This was work. Twenty minutes in I was drenched in sweat and gasping for air. Dad thought I was joking when I asked to take a break, as he was doing fine. After a brief stop, we pushed on. Tiring out so quickly should have been my first indication that something was not right.

We continued to rapidly gain elevation until the trail leveled out and meandered through an old growth forest. The river, whose base would be our home, greeted us with a distant roar. I was ready to collapse. Munching on a bit of food, I suggested we abandon reaching our base camp tonight. Ever congenial, Dad agreed. Twenty-five feet from the trail, we found a ledge overlooking the thunderous stream some one hundred feet below. This was to be our temporary quarters. We hadn't seen another person all day and were sure to sleep undisturbed.

I have had this strange problem with my heart since I was a teenager. I would be sitting calmly, reading a book, when *boom!* suddenly my heart would start racing upward of two hundred beats per minute. This would usually last for about half an hour, and it didn't really bother me except when I was trying to do some physical activity and had to sit down. My condition had baffled doctors. They told me that when I was older it would be my cause of death, as an aged heart was unable to handle that kind of stress.

While navigating the ledge to fill our water supply, my heart began its abnormal pounding. I wasn't concerned, as it was a common occurrence. But after an hour, I became worried. By dusk my heart had been racing for over two hours. I ate a meager dinner and tried to go to sleep. I spent the entire night awake in a state of panic as my heart pounded over the roaring stream. At first dawn, I woke Dad and told him of my plight. He noticed that I was having difficulty with my speech. I was apparently unable to formulate a complete sentence. When he saw that I was incapable of recounting the mountains we were going to climb and the current month, my dad knew something was horribly wrong.

"Nate, we have to get you out of here!" shouted Dad, looking up from his first aid book.

The noise of the river swallowed his voice. I crawled closer to Dad. "What?"

"Nate, you need to go down the mountain!" he pleaded. "I think it's the altitude."

"Really?" I whispered inquisitively. "Okay, give me a few minutes and I'll collect my stuff."

"Leave your stuff here. I'll take care of it. Go now!"

"Are you sure?"

"Yes! Just walk!"

My heart beat away. I could barely stand. Dad lifted me to his shoulder, and shoved a phone in my pocket. With the assistance of my trekking pole, I hobbled toward the trail.

"You might a get phone signal farther down. If so, call 911. If the walking is too much, sit down and wait for me. I'll pack things up and be right there."

His instructions were muffled by the overpowering river, which had long since stopped sounding peaceful. I staggered down the mountain to certain death.

Through the years, I have had a series of prolonged moments when I honestly thought I might die. This was one of them. Each time my thoughts and emotions about death were different. "This would be a good place to die," I mumbled to myself. I would be going out on top, sober and not hurting anyone and doing what I loved. I smiled at the thought that my Abba lay around the bend. The mountains were stunning, and little purple flowers dotted the trail. I reached for one and tumbled over. I chuckled.

Time was lost to me. Dad brought me water and threw his pack on the ground, asking about the phone signal. "I'm going back for your pack. Just keep moving. I'll be back soon." He wasn't interested in the flowers.

Caught between sleep and delirium, I noticed a stranger pouring water in my mouth. His fingers waved at my eyes as he asked a series of questions I was unable to answer. Resting me on his shoulder, he dragged me down the mountain. We had now spent almost twenty-four hours in a vaguely charted woods, and the only person we saw the entire time was an EMT on vacation. Hussein was Trail Angel Number Three.

Somewhere during the steep descent, my heart slowed down. The more elevation we lost, the more consciousness I gained. Soon I was able to stand on my own feet and speak a complete sentence. By the time we reached the parking lot, I was a bit dazed but fully functioning. I was experiencing High Altitude Cerebral Edema: extreme altitude sickness. Treatment was lower elevation and rest.

Hussein sat on the gate of his truck heating soup as we drove away. I will never forget him.

A prolonged nap at a lower elevation was restorative. My gratitude for being alive shifted to sadness at the realization that I had to stay at low elevation. The trip was over.

◆　◆　◆

My father is one of the most accepting people I have ever known. He has adjusted to a series of mishaps and limitations in his life without thought of complaint. I for one had surely at times been a great disappointment. While I have known my dad to micromanage affairs, overreact to small things and respond in anger, he lives the bulk of his life like a quiet stream of water, moving gently in a prescribed path and offering little resistance to life's struggles and frustrations. As a teenager I once pushed my father repeatedly and scoured him with insults. He never struck back. I thought he was weak. And yet as I consider it now, it strikes me that while a stream of water might appear quiet and still, water remains the most powerful force in the natural world.

I like things to go the way I want. Yet I don't trust that I really know what's going to be best for me. Just how do I accept the things I cannot change? Acceptance challenges my perceived notions of control. I couldn't change the fact that I was unable to drink or the fact that we weren't going backpacking. A year of sobriety and time spent with my father had taught me to be grateful for what I had and to accept what I didn't. This much I *did* have control over. In my meetings I was told that I didn't need to settle for anything less than life had to offer. But I did need to accept life on life's terms, and in so doing I would be free to live and learn from the adventures life offers, both good and bad. I had no idea how to do that. My defects of character, which had compelled my self-destructive behavior, were far from resolved. Yet I was sampling that enticing force that motivates the world to leave bed each morning: hope.

15

RISING AND FALLING TO ASSUMPTIONS

ON A LOW ALTITUDE PARK BENCH, I scoured the map. Ditching the rest of our commemorative trip just felt wrong.

"Dad, I feel great. Let's have another go."

"No way! Earlier today you almost died, and now you want to go back up? You're nuts!"

"But what's there to see in Colorado below six thousand feet?" I pleaded.

Watching and dissecting movies together was one of our favorite pastimes, so Dad suggested, "Let's just stay here and watch movies all week."

"We can watch movies anytime. This is our chance. There has to be *somewhere* we can go."

"There's not," Dad said authoritatively.

"You're such a pessimist."

"And you're mad! You should rest."

I smiled and continued to stare at the map.

"What's the elevation of Black Canyon?" asked Dad eagerly. I quickly flipped the pages of the topography map. "It's a meager seven thousand feet and even lower in the canyon." Dad smiled. I danced.

The four-hour drive to the canyon was filled with the same excitement of the previous day. Our trip was being revived. Over the barren high plains we drove. The car was welcome protection from the hot dusty winds as our conversations began. Dad was seeking my opinion about his long-term career plans. His public life was approaching its end.

"Dad, you can't quit until you've been a guest on Larry King," I told him.

"I would love to be asked," he said. I had struck a nerve. His eyes lit with passion. In a serious tone he continued, "Nate, do know how fun it would be to get the phone call from the network . . . and then tell them no?" He cracked a smile and whispered, "I bet no one ever does."

I laughed. I couldn't believe what I was hearing. "And you think *I'm* nuts! You would seriously say no?"

He nodded. "Unless I had some good reason not to."

"Okay, how about Oprah?" I asked. "You have to love Oprah."

"Why on earth would I want to be on those shows?" he replied.

I searched for the answer. "I don't know. I guess everyone does."

"Not me. I can't think of any beneficial reason. People think being on TV means something. Any idiot can be on TV. Go do something stupid and you'll be all over the nightly news. It's not like five minutes on some show is going to help anyone."

I laughed and laughed. He was stuck-up, in his own humble, rebellious way. He was also right; it didn't really matter. He was deliberately trying to avoid the great cultural prize of fame. I totally admired this.

Driving past Blue Mesa Reservoir, we continued our conversation. Dad described for me a series of different ideas of how and when to retire, I gave him my opinions and they seemed to have an effect. I couldn't understand why he was asking my thoughts. Was he humoring me? He didn't really value what I thought, did he?

"Nate, I was going to wait until the top of the mountain to give you this, but it looks like this is as high as we're going."

"Oh, that's funny," I replied, reaching out my hand to receive a card.

The card was a collection of thoughts about why he was proud of me. I had heard this before, but today something was different. It must have been the combination of my admiring his countercultural stance and his seeking my opinions. A desire awoke in me that had lain dormant for many years: I wanted to make him proud.

This was terrifying.

For years, failure had protected me from dealing with such vulnerable emotions. When failure is part of your identity, you don't worry about letting others down. You know you will, and that's that. But if you're proud of me, then you may start expecting me to be a certain way: that felt like a setup. I guess I believed the notion that I was going to go through my life being the only person who didn't care what his parents thought of him. This was turning out to be a bizarre day.

❖ ❖ ❖

Early that evening we rolled into the Black Canyon of Gunnison National Park, set up camp and watched a short video at the visitors' center. As a child I wanted to be a park ranger, so whenever I see one, I find a reason to talk to him or her. They're usually eager to help, and I relish the chance to get a close view of their cool outfits.

"Can you hike into the canyon from here?" I asked the current ranger, studying the symbols on her hat.

"Not now," she said. "It's very technical. We have a number of overlooks and nice day hikes on the rim." She was an uptight ranger.

"How technical?"

"It's getting dark and a rainstorm is on its way." She was clearly annoyed with me. This made me want to talk to her even more.

"Sure, but how technical are we talking?"

Trying to look busy, she reluctantly responded, "There's an old rusty chain you use to climb down the rocky cliffs. It involves a series of dangerous handholds and footholds. The trail really should be closed. We don't advertise its existence. We would prefer not to rescue you on the side of a cliff. You must sign a waiver before you're allowed to access the trail." She had no idea how appealing she just made this.

"Can we go tonight?"

"No, it would be dark before you reached the bottom."

"Sure he can!" barked an older ranger, coming out of his office.

"Bill, they can't climb up the chain in the dark. Besides, it's going to storm any minute," pleaded the uptight ranger.

Bill looked us up and down. We were dirty and eager. "Got headlamps?"

"Yes, sir. Waterproof pants, jackets and boots as well."

"Ah, they'll be fine. Just sign this." He opened an old file cabinet and pulled out a waiver. My uptight friend wasn't done yet.

"In my professional opinion, I would in no way recommend you taking this trail, especially in the dark during a thunderstorm."

The older ranger had set the bar. He believed in us. In the morning I was dying, by afternoon we were going home, and tonight we were embarking on a great adventure. Funny what happens when you accept life on life's terms.

Quickly Dad and I dressed in rain attire and packed hats, gloves, water and food. Headlamps intact, we walked across the mesa toward the canyon and the chain. There was a spring in our steps. We were like little boys exploring an old fort in the woods. Near the edge we encountered a group of people peering into the canyon.

One man asked, "You're not going down in the canyon, are you?"

Like a Southern cop from an old TV show, I confidently responded, "Yes, sir, we are. Bill thinks we can."

"What?" he replied.

I smiled and continued.

Dad shrugged his shoulders and whispered, "Who's Bill?"

Leaving the bushy mesa top, we followed a series of switchbacks that rapidly descended into the canyon. The trees were lush and the dirt was moist. Over a sequence of small cliffs rested the giant chain. The idea was to hold onto the chain and rappel down the cliff by using your feet to walk against the canyon wall. It was much easier than it looked or sounded. The chain was located in a steep gully on the canyon wall that was clearly a runoff during heavy rains and spring snow melt.

"Not too bad," I shouted, bouncing on the chain.

"Yeah, wait until dark," replied Dad. Thunder growled on the mesa top.

"No, wait until the rain washes down this gully. We'll be stuck hanging onto the chain. At least it will be dark and we won't see how far we have to fall!" I shouted back from the swinging chain. Dad was nervous. I couldn't have been happier.

We were greeted at the bottom by the canyon's carver: water. The river echoed a hasty goodbye as she poured downstream. Her power was destined to be harnessed. Vegas needed to be lit. The sun steadily retreated from the upper crust of the black walls, and soon darkness would govern. We soaked our feet in the water as the canyon walls became shadows against the night sky.

The journey up was all I expected it would be: tough, scary and wet. Soldiering on through the sprinkles of rain, I occasionally heard laughter from Dad and his usual remarks about how I was trying to kill him.

"You know we could have done this tomorrow in the daylight when it was dry!" he shouted.

"Ah, Dad, that wouldn't be any fun!"

As the rain passed, a sparkling mass of stars lit the sky. Living in the city, I seldom got to see just how littered the sky could be. In no hurry, we rested. I found a rock that comfortably fit the contours of my underside, turned off my headlamp and stared at the stars. Spontaneously Dad began a story.

It seems that long before my father actually began writing, he secretly dreamed of one day authoring a book. He told this dream to no one, however; not even to my mom. Then one day he was praying with a veteran missionary friend, a man of unusual discernment and wisdom. Laying his hands on my father, this wise old missionary began praying a deep, power-filled prayer. "I pray," he declared, "for the hands of a writer!" My dad's friend had just spoken openly the secret desire of my father. This friend had seen something in my father and given him permission to risk. Dad took this experience as a quiet affirmation for him to pursue the very thing he was too shy to verbalize for himself: a ministry of writing.

It would be nice to say that he achieved because he believed in himself, or because he had the ingenuity and self-determination that it took to succeed, that he pulled himself up by his boot-straps. Yeah, that would be nice. But it wouldn't be true at all. That's hero talk. That's American folklore.

My father became a writer not only because he worked hard, but because he had a supportive community who believed in him, and together they asked God for a gift.

◆　◆　◆

The next day I slept past noon. Dad was stirring a powdery de-light into boiling water. Breakfast was four-cheese chicken enchi-ladas. There is something grand about backpacking food. I assume that if I ate this food at home it would taste awful, but in the woods it's a savory treat.

Resting by a warm fire, we felt a gentle rain begin to fall. Dad began a series of questions, seeking my opinion on various people and issues. We talked for hours. Again, my opinion seemed to matter to him. Why? I was the angry nonconformist who hated the world. Why would he bother with what I thought or said?

I was starting to see how we create worth by what we value, and my dad valued me.

◆ ◆ ◆

Our camp was at the foot of the canyon's southeastern end. Fully aware that yesterday's adventure could not be topped, we opted for a gentle day hike along the river. I had brought a twenty-foot section of climbing rope and a couple of carabiners, and was secretly determined to use both. We found a narrow path that hugged the water's edge and often disappeared. The high river had clearly reclaimed large sections of the path and abruptly ended at a wall of rock. The wall contained the roaring river on its right and formed a high ledge to its left some fifty feet above.

"Looks like we've exhausted the trail. It's over those rocks or across the stream," Dad said, clearly content with this being the end.

"I say we do both! Don't you want to know what it looks like on top of the ledge?"

"No, I don't," he stated resolutely.

"Look Dad, I'll climb up and hold that tree. You can use the rope. It'll be fun."

"It won't be fun."

"We can do it!" I urged.

After a few moments of pondering, Dad responded, "If you say so, I'll take your word for it. I can't believe the stuff you talk me into. If your mother knew what I was doing . . ."

With much effort we scaled the canyon wall, using our weight as leverage. Standing some two hundred feet above the water, we determined it would be best to take a relatively easy route down to the water rather than to return the way we came. This would require forging the river to a path on the other side and crossing again near our campsite. Dad was having fun and agreed.

Lashed together waist-deep in the roaring river, we navigated its frigid current. My trekking poles wobbled violently in the undertow. We approached a chest-deep section of water. To keep from being swept away, we used our strength to support each other with the rope. It was freezing and thrilling. It was also completely clear just how much we needed each other.

◆ ◆ ◆

Dr. Chris Wilgers is a gifted counselor with whom I worked for several years. I once asked why his clients seemed to do so well. He told me that when someone walks in his door, he begins to pray that God shows him who this person could be if they were healed. Rather than asking God what is wrong with the person, Chris asks about his or her potential. Once a picture starts to form, he has this unique way of praying the transformation into the person. He treats the person as if they were fully whole.

We become what others expect us to be. Dad expected me to get better and even assumed I would have something helpful to say. Funny how we rise and fall to the assumptions of others.

16

WHAT'S IN A NAME?
(THE TALE OF SKIPPY AND PETE)

"RICHARD WORKS FROM HIS HOME out in the woods, hikes every day and reads old books by the fire. His life *is* a sabbatical!" joked one of my father's friends, upon hearing of my dad's sixtieth birthday plans for a summer sabbatical.

The statement was true but not complete. Travel was starting to take its toll on my dad, and health problems were beginning to emerge. A two-day speaking trip could wipe him out for a week. Spending a couple of weeks in Korea or England would mean a month to fully recover. My father is a genuine introvert. It's not that he's socially awkward or dislikes people, but just as an extrovert needs other people to gain energy, an introvert needs solitude. It doesn't help that he seems to think that it is his responsibility to be gregarious and witty. Few people understand just how much he has sacrificed to speak around the world. Those who know him well understood that this sabbatical was extremely important.

❖   ❖   ❖

The Continental Divide Trail covers the spine of the Rockies from Canada to Mexico. Dad's sabbatical plan was to backpack the Colorado section of the trail, all seven hundred and eighty miles of it. Dad began hard-core training. All through the winter, he kept a log of his hiking and swimming. He even started lifting weights, although he would quickly clarify that he had no ambitions to be a greased-up muscle man. My father devoured all the information he could find on hiking this newly constructed, relatively unknown trail. He decided to divide the trip into weeklong sections and to use post office boxes to send food and supplies along the way. He spent numerous days at local outfitters, meticulously piecing together the ideal tools for his journey. He weighed and researched everything. My mom remarked that she had never before known Dad, Mr. Simplicity, to spend money on himself, except for books (which don't really count).

❖   ❖   ❖

I discovered that in my brokenness, I made a decent counselor. Propelled by my new master's degree, I started a private counseling practice and watched it grow at an unheard-of pace. Within months I was booked solid. It was tempting to ditch my work and journey with Dad the entire summer, but this was my season of responsibility and family life. I did agree, however, to do the first and last weeks of the journey with him. He recruited others to cover a couple of the weeks, but he would do most of the miles solo. My admiration for what he was doing was unyielding.

Through the winter, Dad would drive down and take Christy and me out for Mexican food. Over enchiladas we processed his upcoming journey.

"Nate, you have to teach me how to tie knots when we get out on the trail. I have this pamphlet, but I can't figure it out." Dad had seen me tie a knot once and assumed I had nautical tying skills. I was happy to oblige. The two simple knots I knew would take him weeks to learn. I just might be able to run the sailor charade all summer.

Licking chip salt from his finger, Dad's tone shifted to a serious one. "Nate, now if I'm going to do this, I want to do it right. I'm planning this trip down to the finest detail. I have weighed everything on the small scale."

"You mean the cocaine scale that measures in hundredths of a gram?"

"Oh, stop it. I've shaved every ounce I possibly can, save for cutting my toothbrush handle. I even have a lightweight pee cup I borrowed from the doctor's office for that late night necessity."

"You planning on returning that borrowed cup there, Dad?" I smarted back, temporarily breaking his tone.

"Now, now, listen up!" he said. "This is serious. I am missing one thing and I need your assistance." I straightened up and listened intently. Christy bore a half-grin; she knew that Dad and I tend to take our mountain adventures entirely too seriously. Dad leaned in, dipped his head and lowered his voice to almost a whisper. "On the Appalachian Trail, through-hikers all carry what's known as a 'trail name.' This is the only name they use when on the trail. You could camp for weeks with a person and only know them as Night Walker or Chef. Nate, I need a trail name. On our first week out, I want you to give me one."

Matching Dad's seriousness, Christy began, "No. I've got it. It just came to me. I have the perfect names for you both." She paused. Then, copying Dad, she leaned in and began to whisper, "You will be . . . Skippy and Pete. Those are your names." She burst into laughter. "Trail names! You two are like children in a clubhouse."

"Hey! Hey!" Dad barked, reaching for esteem on the edge of laughter. It was of no use.

◆　◆　◆

However funny the idea of Skippy and Pete tracing though the woods was, a task had been laid before me. I was to name my father.

In our culture, we usually name kids based on the sound or professional image the name will portray. Parents run potential names through a battery of grade-school songs, weighing the potential for crude nicknames (something my grandparents apparently failed to do when naming my father).

I like how the Israelites named children for what they hoped the person would become. Meanings were always symbolic and significant. These are the meanings I found for our names:

Nathan: gift from God

Lee: protecting shelter, pasture or meadow

Richard: powerful ruler

James: supplanter, one who takes the place or moves into the position of another

Foster: to promote the growth or development of, encourage, nurture; guardian of the forest

I once heard it said that we grow into our names. I'm rather fond of the "Guardian of the Forest" bit. It brings images of a park ranger or some bearded forest dweller chained to an old-growth tree about to be cut down. However, I have never liked the idea of being a gift. I tend to favor receiving over giving.

◆　◆　◆

It was early June when our winter plans became reality. I was on my way to spend the first week of backpacking with Dad. North of Steamboat, Colorado, snaking curves separated rolling hills. On the edge of a river, well-crafted, simple homes sparsely dotted the landscape. A hazy rain painted everything with mystery. Through dense woods, we followed a battered dirt road to its end: Wyoming. Hiking a quarter of a mile up a scant trail, we found our marker. Nailed to a tree was a blue and white triangle with the silhouette of a steep mountain and the letters "CDT," for Continental Divide Trail. This was the entrance to my father's seven-hundred-and-eighty-mile trek. Ziggy led the way as we wrestled with our backpacks.

At the beginning of a long hike, I'm usually a bit nervous and excited. The two emotions lend themselves to good conversation. Ernest Shackleton launched my verbiage. In his pursuit to be the first human to cross Antarctica via the South Pole, he watched his ship rip apart in the frozen ocean. It was 1914, and Shackleton's entire crew was stranded on marine ice miles from any civilization. After twenty-two months at sea, everyone survived by crossing eight hundred miles in lifeboats and then walking across the frozen island. While Shackleton never made it to the South Pole, he does bear the distinction of number one "Ultimate Survivor," according to *Backpacker* magazine. After watching a film about his life, Dad and I agreed to read different books about his five journeys to Antarctica and compare notes.

"Certainly this guy was driven. To continue, failure after failure," I commented.

"Driven! He was stupid," Dad remarked. "How many times do you have to nearly die to realize that maybe you should do something else?"

"And did you catch that he had something like five kids?" I asked. "I realize this guy was an incredible adventurer, but what kind of father could you be if you took trips for two years at a time?"

"You can't," Dad immediately responded.

"So what does that say about him?"

"That he was selfish," he fired back.

Dad and I spent the next hour of our hike analyzing the lives of influential Christian men, both current and historic. With limited data, we tried to assess just how well famous people bore the name "Father." It was becoming clear to us that the history of evangelical men was largely a story of men who ditched their families. My thoughts raced. Maybe the Pauline idea of being single, or at least childless, needed to be readdressed. Was it possible to do significant work and be a family man as well? Did God ever call people to discard their familial responsibilities and not be involved in raising their kids?

I once heard an ultra-conservative guy, who had built his ministry empire on the proselytizing of "family values," give his pseudo-retirement address. Apparently, after spending years of working at the ministry sixty to eighty hours per week, he had decided that it was time to slow down. Even at retirement, however, he seemed completely unaware of the notion that he may have spent more time focusing on his work than his own family. He was championing the value of being a workaholic.

"Don't look so surprised, Nate. It's easy to do. I know I could have done better. I didn't know how to balance family with work and travel. I should have been around more."

I silently nodded my head and smiled. His confession was soothing. It had always been a confusing wound for me. At age thirteen, I had felt like the adults I smoked pot with knew more about my dreams and interests than my own father. He had been busy doing God's work. It didn't help matters that I had acted like I didn't want or need him. Now I wish he would have pushed through my rebellion.

These days I was ready to forgive. I probably already had. Sometimes the spoken word sets us free. Sometimes I need to hear things to put them away, like reading the names of the dead before they are buried.

❖   ❖   ❖

Late afternoon the trail ascended a high ridge. The elevation was near twelve thousand feet. Vegetation was sporadic. As we began to look for a place to camp, we realized something frightening: we had yet to see any water. The Continental Divide is the backbone of North America, dividing rivers between the Pacific and Atlantic oceans. All the rivers to its west dump into the Pacific, and to its east the Atlantic. Somehow, in all the planning, we had missed the meaning of the name and its logical implication that water may be scarce. It didn't help matters that Colorado was experiencing an extreme drought. Things were so dry that forest fires had been popping up all across the state. We spent hours scouring the map and landscape for any sign of water, but to no avail. It was hot. My clothes were drenched in

135

sweat, and I was becoming concerned that we might be in trouble. By nightfall, we each had half a bottle of water left. Before drifting to sleep, I told Dad not to drink more than a couple of swallows through the night.

❖ ❖ ❖

As I lay in my sleeping bag looking at the stars, my thoughts drifted to the earlier conversation. I don't know what it means to be the son of Richard J. Foster, the evangelical superstar. It's good and bad, a myriad of emotions I don't know how to touch or articulate.

When I was younger, people seemed to think they knew something about my world because they had read one of my dad's books. Maybe they did know something, but since I never gave that information, it felt like a sort of violation. I just wanted to run away from anyone who knew what my dad did. It probably didn't help matters that I am a fairly closed person, with a propensity toward paranoia. I've lied about being his son many times.

The Renovaré office recently received a letter from an old classmate of mine:

> After attending a Renovaré conference, I was wondering if Richard has a son named Nathan who attended Northwest High School in Wichita, Kansas. If so, could you give Nathan my contact information? He always said his father was a lumberjack, so I'm not sure I have the right person. Thanks.

I had thought a Kansas lumberjack was a hard sell. Apparently not.

I don't know much about Richard J. Foster. But I really like hanging out with my dad. After all, what's in a name?

17

CHOICES ON THE CONTINENTAL DIVIDE

I WAS SEVEN WHEN DAD TOOK ME to a run-down strip mall to purchase new shoes. Digging through a bin of assorted sneakers, I was unable to decide which ones would make me run the fastest. Dad informed me that in some countries, many people only have two pairs to choose from. He wasn't offering a lesson on gratitude, but rather on the freedom of limited choice—in other words, I wouldn't miss what I didn't know about. It sounded awful. I was already endeared to the materialism that capitalism depends on to survive. In one of his books, Dad referred to our modern accumulation of goods as psychotic. I thought his lack of interest in the latest and greatest was psychotic. For Dad, shunning materialism and the prestige of branding was a spiritual act.

Virtually nothing around my home when I was growing up belonged exclusively to my father. He rode an old bike and wore secondhand clothes. For the sake of simplicity, he took the bus to work every day. When our family did decide to purchase a second car, Dad chose a vehicle with exactly the same layout as our first so that he wouldn't have to learn how to work everything. The word "simplify," spoken in a deep and dramatic tone, was another comical mantra in my home growing up. Dad would voluntarily limit the choices he had in order to live a simple life. I thought he was weird. I was extremely entertained by the latest technology, and I had a propensity for hoarding things.

Now, however, as an adult, I had a garage full of junk that seemed to own me. My garage was leading me to reevaluate my father's choices as potentially insightful and clever.

◆ ◆ ◆

"Nate, you up yet?" my dad called out the next morning.

"No, I'm not. Leave me alone."

"Just toss me your water bottle, sleeping beauty!" Dad joked.

"What? Where's yours?"

"I drank it."

I jolted up. "You did *what?!*"

"Oh, stop it. I got thirsty. Throw me your water."

Shaking my head, I scolded him, "You haven't seen thirsty yet!"

"You're supposed to drink lots at high elevation," he whined in defense.

"Just wait until you're carrying a fifty-pound pack uphill at this elevation."

"Oh, we'll find water," he said with shaky confidence.

"And what if we don't?"

This was probably the first and last time that I handled a situation with more caution and conservation than my father.

"Well, if you're not going to give me any water, how about some extra toilet paper?"

"You didn't bring toilet paper?"

"No, I did. I counted out the squares and weighed them. And now I think I'm going to run out."

"You weighed your toilet paper? So just how much does toilet paper weigh?"

"Oh, stop it. Give me some toilet paper!"

"Wow, that would be a good lesson in making better choices, wouldn't it?"

"What? You're not going to give me any?" Dad pleaded.

"I'm a firm believer in natural consequences." I rolled over to go back to sleep. He burst out laughing, mumbling something about how I couldn't be serious.

Breakfast was stiff bagels dipped in peanut butter. I reluctantly shared a few sips of water with my dad, since letting him eat peanut butter without water was just too malicious. Besides, guarding my toilet paper would be punishment enough. It was 9:00 a.m., and the sun was pounding down. Twelve ounces of water left meant a cruel agony lay ahead.

We journeyed for seven miles up and down through woods and rock. By mid-afternoon, only a few swallows of water were left. As the sun reached its pinnacle, the shade abandoned us. We were over two miles above sea level and still had to climb five hundred more feet on a barren hill carrying nearly fifty pounds each. My muscles and head ached as dehydration set in. I would have been happy to stop and set up camp, but without water there was no point. I feared another thirsty night more than the dizziness and pain. Ziggy was limping. His long tongue was dry.

"Where's some freaking water?" I shouted.

"I don't know, Nate. I shouldn't have drunk that water last night," Dad confessed.

"I know!" I grumbled. "Hey, you might want to grab some of those leaves," I mumbled as I passed him to lead the uphill march.

"Why?"

Without turning around I shouted back, "I assume you're going to have to use the bathroom. Dehydration causes diarrhea."

"Hey! Wait a minute. I've had about enough of that. You're going to share, aren't you?" he whimpered.

The next two hours were a blur of fear and pain, but we trudged on. I was beginning to question whether or not we would ever run into water until Ziggy came strolling back to us from where he had run ahead. Black mud encased his shaggy fur. Why is it that when hope fades, life seems to turn around?

"Dad, look at Zig!"

"Oh! What a mess. He's not sleeping in the tent tonight."

"Dad, it's *mud!* Where there's mud, there's water!"

"You're right! Come on, Zig! Show us the way!" he shouted.

Wearing a big dog smile, Ziggy wove through a series of trees that led to a grassy clearing. A quarter of a mile past the open expanse was a muddy swamp. I fell to the ground with delight, hugging Ziggy. It's horribly difficult to pump muddy water through a filter, but at this point it was sheer joy. We would camp here. Before sundown we were all asleep.

❖   ❖   ❖

The afternoon sun bled through the tent. It must have been one hundred degrees in my down cocoon.

"Ready to hit the trail?" I shouted, snuggling my pillow.

"Sure," came Dad's voice from outside the tent.

"You don't sound convinced," I replied.

"I'm not sure your dog's up for any more. I can't get him to move." Dad was practicing knots. Ziggy lay collapsed in his lap.

"Come here, boy!" I pleaded. "Ziggy, come here!" I said again. He smiled, but didn't budge. As if to explain his disobedience, he began licking his cracked paws.

"Look what you did to your dog," Dad said, only half joking. "His paws are in bad shape."

It was true: Ziggy's paws were obviously hurting. "Well, it looks like this will be home for a while," I announced, to the unspoken relief of us both.

"Nate, come see this place. We're in a stunning meadow."

Somehow, in the exhaustion of the previous day, I had missed how picturesque our oasis was. We were camping on the edge of a lush meadow, hidden from the trail by a grove of trees. Green grass sprinkled with an array of flowers stretched for a good mile. The swampy meadow was unevenly encapsulated by trees. Gentle Wyoming peaks framed the backdrop.

This was my own secret garden. "I felt the green veil creeping over the world, and the soft wind blow down from the mountains" (*The Secret Garden*, Francis H. Burnett).

The Spirit of God resided unhindered in this place.

In the western American wilderness, far from any trail, I might just be the first human to set foot on any particular patch of earth.

Chances are that we were the only people who would ever see the landscape in this exact form. The flower in front of me would die before another person passed this way. Who knows? The whole forest could burn down before the week was over. I like to think that God had put this ever-changing landscape here for my enjoyment. For three days we soaked in the magic. I only moved to use the bathroom or pump mud. Ziggy never moved.

Between knot-tying and stick-carving, my father and I talked. I discovered that he knew nothing about the music and movies of his youth. He had shunned popular culture as a quiet way of making a stand. I also learned about his dissertation on the Quakers' stance against slavery and that he visited the Black Panthers office.

Even Renovaré had a hint of the countercultural. He had no desire for it to become large. In his office, he kept a model corporate jet with the Renovaré inscription on it. Someone had given it to him as a joke, and it served to remind him what the organization was *not* to become. Contrary to the common practice, he chose board members based on their talents and skills rather than their ability to financially contribute to the organization. He crossed denominational, racial and gender lines and placed a diverse group of gifted people at the helm.

The main goal of Renovaré was to equip churches to offer a balanced vision of spiritual formation—"like Samson lighting the tails of the foxes and letting them run," he explained (Judges 15:4-5). Instead of pursuing large venues, Renovaré put on multiple conferences per year, usually held by small churches. In order to host a conference, a church had to work with other local congregations. Dad smiled as he told of the relationships that were developed between neighborhood churches that had never spoken to each other before. He got a kick out of that kind of thing.

For hours I probed his intellect. I had once thought of my father as uptight, but much to my surprise, I found that I shared many of the same values and ideas. As the days wore on, Dad was proving extremely interesting to talk with. Each day we used Ziggy's recovery as an excuse to stay in the meadow, and each day I refused to share my toilet paper.

The thrashing delivered by the Continental Divide Trail was forcing Dad to rethink his summer goal. Each day, he was becoming more aware of his limits. Ultimately, he decided to abandon his plans to tackle the entire trail and opted to complete the more scenic sections. Dad chose the path of wisdom and let go of a goal he had spent the entire year working toward with astounding grace. He knew who he was. My father accepted himself and what he could accomplish in a spirit that left me envious.

I could have stayed in the meadow for weeks. My heart vibrated with peace. This was the first time since I had gotten sober that I had really stopped to rest. Staying busy helps to distract, but it has its consequences. In that meadow, I lost a lot of anxiety I'd been wearing. Simple phrases and ideas have been some of my greatest teachers, although sometimes they take years to soak in. This week I was left with a profound sense that God never calls me to a life of hurry. I choose it.

Time dictated that we would travel no further. Tomorrow we would head back to the car. I guess turning around could be seen as failure, but this wasn't. It was marvelous. Not accomplishing our goal meant nothing. That last night in the meadow we slept under the stars, watching bats fly just above our heads.

Packing as much filtered mud as we could carry, we headed back toward the car. We stopped for lunch in the shade of a large tree and feasted on crunchy bagels and now slimy peanut butter. Oddly, our food actually seemed to increase in its desirability as the days wore on. While Dad messed with his backpack, I climbed to an overlook in hopes of finding a phone signal. It was wonderful to talk with my wife. Absence can make a struggling marriage feel strangely nostalgic.

While on the phone, I noticed a small billow of smoke in the distance. Fifteen minutes later that billow had not only grown, but it was significantly closer. I hung up the phone and shouted to Dad, pointing to the smoky sky. Within seconds Dad had gathered his stuff and was heading along the trail. I scampered down the rock side to meet up with him.

Handing him the phone, I started running back to the place we had eaten lunch to get my backpack. "Call 911 if you get any signal. I'll catch up with you."

"Are you sure you should go for your pack?" he hollered.

"Don't worry. I'll run," I shouted back.

By the time I got my pack and caught up to him, the fire was raging. Visible flames engulfed the trail just half a mile behind us. Our magical meadow was clearly ablaze. Dad had reached 911 and gave the location of the fire.

"Dad, when the flames reach that tree where we ate lunch, we toss the packs and run!" I said. He agreed.

In a matter of moments planes came, dumping water on the forest behind us. We were now hiking uphill, moving at a grueling pace. Dad placed another call to the Forest Service.

"How about you send someone to get us?" Dad asked, after giving the operator our location. The woman continued to ask Dad a series of unimportant questions, clearly trying to keep him on the phone.

"Dad, it's time," I said impatiently. "We need to run!"

He continued on the phone.

"Dad, hang up!" I yelled.

"But she told me to stay on the line."

"I don't care. Give me the phone and run!" I glanced back at the dark red flames dancing in the sky. "Look ma'am, I'm going to hang up the phone," I told the operator. "We need to run."

"Sir, I need you to calm down and stay on the line."

"I'm sure you do." I hung up and ran. The top of the hill was the finish line.

Unless a downhill slope greeted us on the other side, we would have to sacrifice the packs so that we could sprint.

At the top of the hill, we found a beat-up truck driven by a drunk guy. Just how he got his truck on the trail was beyond me.

"Hey, what's up, guys?" yelled Trail Angel Number Four out the window of his truck.

"We need a ride!" I shouted, throwing my pack in the back of his pickup.

"Oh, okay. Yeah . . . sure," he slurred. We piled into the truck.

"Hey, you guys mind if we drive to the edge of the fire first?" he asked.

"Yes!" Dad shouted, reaching for the door to get out.

"Okay! Okay! Just checking. I've never seen anything like this before." Grinding the gears and slipping off the trail, the truck sped away.

"Hey! You guys look like you need a beer," the driver told us. "The cooler's behind you."

"Yeah, beer is the last thing I need," I responded, overjoyed to be rescued.

"Well, hand me one. You sure you don't want to see the fire?"

"Yes!" we both shouted.

After reaching a safe distance from the fire, we opted to continue on foot. Peering into the distance, we watched the onslaught of helicopters trying to save the forest. We called Search and Rescue to let them know we made it out and then headed home, grateful to be alive.

There are so few things I have any control over in this world. I live with an artificial sense of power over my destiny while simultaneously throwing away the only real control I have: my daily choices.

I have become convinced that I am a few bad choices away from becoming just about any kind of person. My propensity for destruction remains my greatest fear.

18

ELECTRIC AIR ON HOLY CROSS

WHEN I WAS SIXTEEN YEARS OLD, I worked in Oregon for a summer. I spent my days off alone, wandering through the forest. I gravitated toward the woods by the river and the people who occupied the fragile shanties there. My homeless friends had a sense of community that I envied. I was lonely, yet I wanted to be alone. This dichotomy lingers for me today, although in diminished form.

I'm not sure when my thirst for a sense of community started. It might have been forming a connection with my father, or just the isolation that adulthood seems to bring. Either way, my attention was steadily turning toward building relationships. This stood in stark contrast to the consistent allure of living in the mountains alone. As a teenager, I would have told you that I didn't need human relationships, and I treated others as if this were true. Yet I'm just like most people: lost somewhere in the tension between wanting to know and be known, yet afraid of being hurt or discovered.

"Building and cultivating relationships is the most significant thing you will do on earth": I wish I could remember where I first heard this statement. It's been spinning in my head for years.

◆　◆　◆

That summer I felt change brewing. My work as a counselor was isolating and exhausting. I missed the collective experience of university life.

One day, the summer air beckoned me to the mountains. I wanted to climb. Christy and my daughter Autumn were out of town, and Dad couldn't change his plans at short notice. Besides, Mount of the Holy Cross was a longer hike than Dad would have liked. And with a name like Holy Cross, it only seemed fitting to climb it with God.

The trail was wildly scenic, ascending a thousand feet before descending even more into a narrow wooded valley at the base of a roaring river. I dipped my face in the water, soaking in its frozen glory. I had come to appreciate water sources in the mountains. Yet as much as I enjoyed being alone, I also remembered how much richer life is when you share it with others. The trees seem greener and the mountains higher.

My pace was strong and steady. I summited with surprising ease, amazed at my potential to adapt to difficult challenges. As promised, the summit offered a grand view. I enjoyed it for over an hour.

Slowly, however, I began to notice a slightly nervous breeze blowing about. Growing with intensity and heading my direction, a smudge of blackness began to consume the sky. With unease, I quickly headed down the mountain.

Thirty minutes into my descent I suddenly noticed that my hair, which was well past my chin in length, was floating towards the sky and standing straight out. Simultaneously, my metal poles began to vibrate with electricity. I had read that such phenomena occur just before lightning strikes. My worry shifted to panic, and I quickly threw my poles down the mountain and ran. Thunder cracked, beckoning an onslaught of heavy rain. In my haste, I slipped and fell half a dozen times before the light show began.

The lightning started to my right. I quickly turned and headed to the left. Behind me, light flashed. Suddenly thunder boomed with an instantaneous strike right in front of me; the sound reverberated in my ears. I turned and headed straight down the mountain, but I was still a good two thousand feet from the forest. If I continued to run, it would be an hour until I reached the woods. Lightning struck straight ahead of me, and then immediately to my right.

I finally realized that I was cornered; there was no point in running. In every direction I would face danger. Wet, scraped and bruised, I raised my hands in the air and screamed, "*Ahhhhhh!!* I quit!!"

I found a comfy rock and let the rain beat down.

I'm always running into this conundrum in life: every option seems to hold consequences I'd rather not face. The mantra of the self-proclaimed victim is a familiar one: "Damned if I do. Damned if I don't." So while I often don't like the results I'm getting in any particular situation, change offers no guarantee of better. I'm often immobilized by choices. People sometimes say that my generation is lazy. I think we're scared to fail.

It made no difference what I did; I was going to die.

After a few moments of frustration, for some reason, I let go and accepted the situation. I pulled an apple from my pack and decided to leisurely stroll around through the rain. Somehow, I was suddenly overcome by a blind faith that seemed to come out of nowhere. God was bigger than me; I didn't have to be in control.

◆　◆　◆

He was ten and crying frantically. Some fifty feet away I watched as his dad paced about, desperately trying to coax him down the mountain. Frozen from shock, the child refused to move. I realized suddenly that now I had purpose, one last noble deed before death greeted me. It was my time to be a Trail Angel. I raced toward them confidently, grabbed the child's hand and led them down the mountain. I had no clue where I was going, but to my surprise they followed.

I chose a nearby rock crevice that provided shelter from the rain. We were now actually a bigger target for the lightning, as our bodies provided a connection between the shallow overhang and ground below, but it gave us a sense of protection. Besides, we were all going to die anyway. The boy was shivering uncontrollably from the wet cold. I produced dry clothes from my pack and a bag of peanuts.

For the next thirty minutes we watched the lightning dance. I tried to offer a witty commentary on the light show as we marveled at the array of colors found in the flashes. I was particularly fond of discovering a cobalt ball on the end of some lightning bolts. Together the three of us marveled at the power of the storm. This felt like corporate worship.

I thought about my struggle with the fact that as a child, I'd had to share my father with the rest of the world. But maybe I could see my loss as a blessing that I could now freely offer to others. My father's work had been a help to people. Instead of feeling like a victim, maybe I could choose to give my father to the world.

After the storm, the noise of thunder rang in my ears for hours. My body danced with the hum of electricity for over a week. I won't forget sharing peanuts and lightning with that boy and his dad. Being written into the page of someone else's father-son story was redemptive. I needed them as much as they needed me.

19

BEAUTY BEYOND IMAGINATION

Judith Biggles lived at the end of my block. She was old and lonely. Her existence consisted of television, a weekly trip to the grocery store and the hopes of a card from the grandkids. Her house was littered with reminders of who she was: teacher, mother, wife, Christ follower.

It was winter when Judith broke her hip. Unable to call for help, she starved to death in her kitchen. Weeks passed before her body was found. Her kids felt sad, a bit guilty and annoyed with the mess of cleaning up her house. Mrs. Biggles's sense of uselessness was revealed in her scrupulous journal. She had made a semblance of peace with the idea that no one seemed to want her around. This is the story of our elderly.

I recently came across a photograph taken by Kevin Carter. It's a haunting image of a starving toddler crawling in the desert of

Sudan. In the distance a vulture patiently waits for the girl to die. Shortly after winning a Pulitzer Prize for the photograph, Kevin killed himself. Extreme poverty is one-third of our world's story.

Abandonment and death affect us all with unspoken force: the loss of human potential. What love and wisdom did Mrs. Biggles have to give her community? Who could that child crawling in the desert have been? What life did Jesus intend for her? What faces of humanity will go unrecorded because Kevin saw death as his only option?

When the world loses the gifts and blessings of one of its own, it conjures a grief that becomes knit into the spiritual fabric of our souls. Lost potential is the byproduct of every evil in this world.

I wasn't prepared for the tears that came when I started asking who we could be as a people. I began to see Jesus' intention for us. It is a beauty beyond imagination. It became clear to me how much we need each other to become the people God intends. Yet we have become what many consider to be the most disconnected society in all of human history.

What happened to the authentic communities that could call us out of our selfish individualistic lives? I wonder what Jesus envisioned by a kingdom of people who serve one another and understand that the first are last.

◆　◆　◆

So exhausted that I wasn't sure what day it was, I locked up my office, breathed in the night air and drove to meet Dad. Counseling others often felt like taking a fifty-minute beating. My lack of mental prowess was evidence of the ten sessions I had endured that day. Even determining my own phone number had become a mental chore. Yet the work was also marvelous, exposing me to incredible grace and beauty in the lives of others.

Dad and I would be at the base of Mount Shavano before midnight, with the goal of summiting in the last hour of darkness. Freeze-dried eggs and sausage awaited us, as did the sun's grand entrance. This was a way to avoid any chance of lightning. Even though it had been a year since my experience on Holy Cross, I was still significantly traumatized.

The temperature at the trailhead was in the low thirties. For late June, this was a welcome chill. The moon hid its glow as clouds hovered about. In silence, we prepared our packs and secured our headlamps. I was nervous and tired. Our midnight quest began with the piercing of eerie shadows.

These past years with my father had sparked an interest in having people in my life. My fierce independence was starting to fade. It didn't help that both Christy and I were still adjusting to being new parents and desperately needed support. As Dad and I found our rhythm in the darkness, the conversation ensued.

"How come we never hung out with other people when I was a kid?" I asked.

"What do you mean?" His confusion was sincere.

"I don't really know any adults from my childhood. And it was rare that we saw any extended family."

"I don't know," my dad responded. "I never really thought about it."

"I really wish I had had older people in my life when I was growing up," I lamented. "What I wouldn't give for a grandparent who had been involved in my life."

"Yeah, I think we let you down on that front," my dad said.

"No worries," I answered. "I'm just jealous of people with large extended families. Wasn't there a time in history when people felt connected and committed to each other? I've lived in the same house for years and never spoken to 90 percent of the people in my neighborhood."

"It's been hard for you guys, hasn't it?" my dad asked with compassion.

"It's been awful. I suck at this parent thing, and we haven't had a date in over a year." Dad nodded. After a bit of thought, he responded, "In the early years I was really interested in living in community."

"You wanted to join a commune?" I said, with baiting mockery.

"No, not really," he growled. "We once tried living with another family as an experiment to maybe do something larger. After that didn't work out, your mom said that I could live in community if I wanted, but that she wouldn't join me." He laughed as he remembered her resolve.

"You mean I could have eaten from a garden composted with baby poop? Oh Dad, you really let me down. I've always had a propensity for patchouli oil and hairy pitted women."

"Oh, stop it," he hammered back. "It wasn't like that at all." Shifting to a more serious tone, he continued, "I think in the past, the church often facilitated a sense of care for people. Social life was oriented around the church."

"Sure, our family went to the same church for years," I said. "But I honestly don't think one person from that place gave a rip about me. The only person I remember was the guy who would yell if I tried to take more than one donut." (I was frustrated and not being completely truthful. The pastor and his family had been extremely loving, but he had died when I was in third grade.)

"I don't know, Nate," my dad said in a sympathetic tone. "People are busy, I guess . . ."

Into the darkness our journey continued. The air had a surreal, dreamlike presence to it. The late-night giggles were starting to set in, and sarcasm was about to get the best of me.

"You know what it is, Dad? It's because evangelical churches want to be like Wal-Mart."

"Wal-Mart? What?" he chuckled.

"I know what you're thinking: I'm going to go off on the idea of how they're both propaganda machines intent on selling a product. You think I'm going to say something about Americans trivializing the holy by reducing the mysteries of God into a slogan or some easy-to-remember acronym. And it's true; just the other day I saw a church sign that read 'Wal-Mart is not the only saving place!' But really, I've got a better connection. Want to hear it?"

"No," my dad teased. "But seeing how I'm stuck with you for the rest of the night, I have a feeling you're going to tell me anyway."

"Come on, Dad! It's good. I've been working on this. So, have you ever noticed that in the midst of the glitz and glamour of Wal-Mart's falling prices, one thing remains missing? Why do you think they hire people with the sole purpose of saying 'Hi!' to you?"

"I don't know, Nate. I never go to Wal-Mart."

"What? Dad, it's an American staple! You get to support the atrocities of China while filling your house with useless junk. You really need to get out more."

"No, I don't." He was clearly entertained by my passion.

"Anyway, the employees wear blue smocks with smiley faces. 'Why?' you may ask. Because they know personal contact is the major deficiency in the big-box consumer industry. The mega-church is forever caught in the same conundrum. The nature of a large structure is cold and impersonal. All the smiley smocks or free coffee in the world can't change that. No matter how wonderful an experience the customer has, it can't match the feeling of personal connection from the old mom-and-pop stores. Now in church, a lot of people don't seem to mind the lack of connection. In fact, many people love the idea that they can go to church and hide in the back. It's like going to the movies. You get that feeling of connection without having to talk to anyone."

"Nate, I hate to tell you, but not every church is a megachurch."

"It's called Wal-Mart envy," I continued.

"Oh, brother. There's more."

"Come on, this is good!" I burst into laughter. Composing myself, I went on. "We've bought the lie of the business world: success is bound to measureable growth, size and numbers. Then mix that lie with insecurity, hide it in the Great Commission, and what you get is our unyielding obsession with numeric growth. Rather than being who we are, building relationships, discipling one another, and celebrating the fact that we have the ability and agility to love and serve others, we sell ourselves out to pursue the prize of Wal-Mart."

"I know," my dad replied. "These days we have become obsessed with the ABCs of church life: attendance, building and cash. You're describing a consumer Christianity that effectively chokes off the life of spiritual formation and any serious discipleship to Jesus."

"Yes. Yes! Wow, and you even threw in an acronym," I replied, impressed.

"Oh, stop it. So you like Wal-Mart, do you?" Dad asked, following my shift back to humor.

"I'd rather go there than church!" I snapped back.

"You're nuts, Nate," he chuckled.

"Yeah, I know."

Our conversation continued as we kept hiking. That night it dawned on me that I had failed to draw any connection between my angry sarcasm and my father's work. He had been quietly working to better the church for years. His life's work had been calling on the church's strengths, calling people together. The man I once saw as an insider was upset too. He was just doing something about it.

Much of who I am today I learned from my dad, yet I didn't know that I was learning from him. He used the most powerful form of education: example.

◆　◆　◆

Because we were hiking in the dark, it was impossible to tell how far we had come. Eventually the sun's pre-glow illuminated the mountaintop. We were still a couple of hours away. I was enjoying myself too much to care. The people passing us laughed when Dad revealed that we had been hiking all night; it was too unbelievable to them that we could be that slow. It wasn't until 10:00 in the morning that we reached the summit. The idea of cooking sausage and eggs had lost its appeal. I opted for a nap.

On the edge of a dream, I heard voices commenting on the darkening sky. I jolted up in fear. A dark haze was consuming the mountain. It was time to go! Within minutes, I felt electricity buzzing in my bones. My body had felt altered since the lightning storm on Holy Cross. I would occasionally feel an electric pulse spinning in my head or tingles shooting down my legs. Years later I would liken it to the feeling you get from having acupuncture.

"Dad, we need to move fast!" I yelled.

"I can't," he said. "My knees will buckle; my ankles are too weak. You go on ahead."

"No, I'll stay with you."

Dad's downhill tempo was nearly as slow as his uphill one. Within thirty minutes, everyone who had been at the summit had trampled past us. Thunder snarled in the distance, announcing a raging downpour.

"Dad, we have to hurry!" I said impatiently.

"Nate, I can't!" he yelled though the pelting rain.

"Try! Falling will be of little concern if we don't hurry."

He tried, and for the next ten minutes we made good distance despite his numerous slips. Each time he got up more unsure of himself than before. After falling against a jagged rock and scraping his leg, he announced his resolve. "Nate, go on ahead. I can't go any faster."

"No. I'll stay with you."

Wind escorted the rain in all directions. It was cold but somehow refreshing. We were vulnerable to the will of the storm. I once again accepted my lack of control and embraced the situation like a naked man deciding to be proud rather than embarrassed. Eventually we made it to the trees. It wasn't really safer, but it felt better. Two parallel paths emerged. Indifferently we strolled through the rain shoulder to shoulder.

Suddenly, in Dad's direction, a blinding light flashed. At the exact same moment, thunder struck like a gunshot two inches from my ear. I looked over at my father. He lay motionless on the ground, curled up in a fetal position.

◆　◆　◆

In the ensuing seconds, my thoughts exploded in rapid succession. Affection for others is a funny thing. Like education and patience, relationships tend to creep up on me with almost no allowance for my awareness. I have found there's nothing quite like a crisis to deliver a solid serving of gratitude.

This wasn't the same man I knew growing up. I used to think he was the one who had changed. Most likely it was me. Our relationship had come to mean more than I ever could have imagined. He was my best friend, and now I was sure he was dead. Panic washed over me, and tears welled up as I rushed to his side.

"Dad! Dad!" I shouted. He didn't respond.

I shook him. His head slid to the side.

"Wow, that was crazy!" he whispered, as if the lightning was listening.

"I thought you'd been hit!" I yelled, pushing him over.

"Yeah, me too!" he laughed, slowing rising to his feet.

"What were you doing on the ground?"

"That thing scared me. I was taking cover," he defended.

"Damn! I thought you were dead!"

"I'm a bit surprised we're not. The lightning must have stuck within a few feet of us."

"I know. Let's get out of here." For some reason, Dad was now able to move at a much faster pace than ever before.

Eventually the storm passed. My shock remained, as did the thunder echoing in my ears. Once again electricity would pulsate in my body for days. This was the first time we were able to see the wooded terrain with more than a headlamp. It was clear that the rain had washed the trail clean. Adrenaline was replaced with exhaustion, and every step became a struggle. Yet my thoughts were on fire. I felt magic brewing in my head.

"Dad, what was it like to teach college?"

"Oh, it was good. I enjoyed it."

After moments of silence, Dad offered a gift. "Nate, you'd be great at teaching."

"You think so?"

"Yeah. Yeah, you would. You know, it may be just what you need. That counseling work seems to be wiping you out."

"Yeah, it is. I was just thinking that working at a university might help give Christy and me a sense of community. This parenting gig is tough."

"I wish we lived closer to you guys."

"Me too."

"Dad, I can't teach. I don't have a tweed jacket with corduroy elbow patches."

"Oh, is that what it takes?"

"I don't know. Seriously, I don't think I could find a job without a Ph.D."

"You never know unless you try. It never hurts to ask."

"Yeah, you're right. But you know it would mean I'd have to leave Colorado. There are only two social work programs in the state and you need a Ph.D. to teach at both."

"You've looked into this," he said, surprised.

"Yeah."

"Leave the state, huh?" His sadness was clear.

Muddy and tired, we reached a footbridge covering a swollen river. We were the first on the mountain and now the last to leave. Leaning my worn body against the railing I realized just how much my father's approval had come to mean to me. Relationships make us vulnerable and needy, and they set us up for hurt. Yet I have a sense there is greater power and strength in embracing the risk.

"Well, Nate, it might be worth it to have a job that works for you," he said with a sort of resolution.

"Yeah, maybe. But I don't think I could stand to leave the state. I love this place."

"I don't know. Maybe Colorado doesn't want you here," he joked. "First the forest fire, then the two lightning storms. Maybe it's time for you to go!"

"Maybe."

20

WALKING EACH OTHER HOME

"NATE, HOW DID IT GO? WHAT DID THEY SAY?" Dad asked on the phone, giddy with anticipation.

"Really well, I think," I answered. "They said they were very interested in me."

"Did you like the town?"

"It's poor and run-down, but covered with beautiful lush trees and rolling hills. They call them mountains, but really they're just hills."

"And the school: what do you think?"

"Fine, just fine. I really want to teach, so I'm easy to please."

"Yeah, sure. So did they say when they'll decide?"

"Next week."

"Oh man, Nate! I'm so excited for you. How was the suit?"

"Awful. But I tied my tie like a dream. Thanks for the lesson."

"Sure. Well, let me know when you hear something. Have a good flight."

I was in southeastern Kentucky. It was everything I'm not: Southern Baptist, rural, and filled with self-proclaimed rednecks and hillbillies who know how to be content with life. Someone described the place to me as Mayberry with a college. The nearest coffee shop was over an hour away. Yet when the offer came, I accepted. For some odd reason, Christy and I couldn't have been more excited. It was a new adventure with my dream job. With extraordinary anticipation and the occasional sadness, we planned the move.

One final mountain was in order. This would be the end to a beautiful string of adventures that had dominated the landscape of my twenties. Mount Audubon was a thirteen-thousand-foot mountain in the Indian Peaks Range that I could see from my office window each day. Over the years, Dad and I had occasionally tried to summit Mount Audubon in the winter. One time we had gotten lost in the snow, and another year we had been unable to locate the trail early enough in the day to summit. We were both determined to finally see the pinnacle of Audubon. It was early summer, so there was no worry of snow (or at least that's what we thought). To extend the trip a bit, we decided to backpack to the base and summit the following day.

Driving into the mountains with the top down on my Jeep was spectacular. The wind and the changing view of the peaks were mesmerizing. That all ended when we were pelted by a freak snowstorm. (There was also an incident in the snow on the side of a normally desolate road involving an upset stomach and the with-holding of toilet paper, but some stories should remain untold.)

We reached the trailhead unsure about the whole thing, as neither of us had brought gear for the snowy blast. After a few miles of trudging through the wet snow, we decided to set up camp and crawl into our sleeping bags for warmth. The snow soon stopped, but the cold lingered. In the tent, Dad was fiddling with a rope and I was writing.

"Nate, show me how to do that knot again."

"What knot?"

"The one you showed me in the meadow."

"What? You mean after that long summer of backpacking you still can't tie that simple knot?!"

"Oh, stop it. It's *hard!*" he defended.

"No it's not!" I laughed.

"Hey, who was thirty and didn't know how to tie a tie? Come on, I'm a slow learner. Just one more time."

"Okay, fine. Hey, I never gave you a trail name, did I?"

"No, but your wife did. I forget, am I Skippy or Pete?"

"You're both. Seriously Dad, I have a name for you."

"All right!" Dad sat up straight and adjusted his shoulders, preparing for his coronation.

"Wisdom Chaser."

"Wisdom Chaser. Hey, I like it. That's a nice name. I thought you were going to say something about my knot-tying skills."

"Well, I kind of am," I replied. "You're slow, but you're teachable. Very few people in this world are teachable—and you're even a doctor. A teachable doctor is unheard of. It may just explain why you have been so successful with the books and whatnot. You work hard to learn. That's wisdom."

"Hey, I like this! Wisdom. Wisdom Chaser." He repeated the

words as if he were trying on a new coat and turning around in the mirror.

"Now the Chaser part is a bit of a joke," I added. "Chasing denotes quickness, and you don't do anything quickly. In fact, you're slow at just about everything from hiking to tying your shoe. And maybe that's not such a bad thing. Most people are trying to do things faster. So here you are, the last intentionally slow man on earth."

"'Last slow man on earth.' Seriously Nate, I'll wear the name proudly."

"Good. I'm glad you like it. It only took two years for me to come up with. I guess your slowness is starting to rub off. Anyway, I'm hungry. Do we have anything to eat that doesn't require going out in the cold and cooking?"

"No. You want to go out and cook?"

"I'm not that hungry! I'm freezing in my sleeping bag!"

"So you're going to let your old dad starve just because you're a little cold?"

"Yep!"

"I can't cook. I'm so slow it may just be tomorrow before I'm finished," he mused.

I stared at the setting sun out of the tent window. Dad kept trying his knot.

"This is crazy!" I bellowed.

"I know. Do you realize how cold it's going to get in here tonight? We're going to freeze!" Dad replied.

"If we leave now, we could make a 9:30 movie. I've got a coupon for free popcorn," I baited.

"Are you serious? Nate, this is your last chance to climb a mountain before you move."

"I've climbed enough mountains. I'm cold."

"A movie it is then!" Dad shouted, smiling with delight.

I had changed. The mountains were about having fun and being together, not about conquest. And so, with a movie, popcorn and great laughter, we ended nearly a decade of climbing mountains together.

◆ ◆ ◆

Dad took great interest in my job and move. He remained a constant source of encouragement, following every detail of the process. When I was applying to various schools, he even offered to use some of his connections at various universities if I thought it would be useful. I was willing to receive any help I could, a fact that marked a huge shift in my thinking. I now knew my dad. We hiked and laughed. Thus, I now felt free to accept my connection to him as a writer and speaker. In the end, it didn't actually matter; Dad knew no one in the backwoods of Kentucky.

Just before the move date, my wife discovered a severely atypical mole on my back. It was apparently well on its way to becoming a melanoma and necessitated the removal of a golf-ball size chunk of flesh. Dad's presence during that time exceeded my expectations; he drove two hours each way for both the consultation and surgery. This must have been especially difficult for him in ways he never expressed; he had witnessed his own brother die from this very disease.

When the time for our move arrived, I was excited, sad and empty all at the same time. Leaving was hard but it seemed right, almost poetic. According to my mom, after we left, Dad passionately sobbed. He wasn't the only one.

Leave it to a nurse-practitioner in a state with horrible heath care to finally discover the source of my rapidly beating heart. "Supraventricular tachycardia" was the name. It was a congenital defect, and there was a surgery to fix it. One month before my son was born, the procedure was scheduled. Christy was on bed rest because of possible pregnancy complications, so I was prepared to go it alone. Against my insistence, Dad flew out to Kentucky and spent two nights in the hospital with me. The nurses must have thought we were crazy; considering the circumstances, we had way too much fun. This was only one more mountain to climb.

That first year of teaching, I worked harder than I ever had before. Fueled by the awareness of my intellectual deficiencies, I labored many a long night. I found a new twelve-step group and continued the journey of staying sober. I mostly hiked alone now, yet never without a thought of my father. I could hardly tie my boots without missing him. Our nine years of climbing mountains together were over.

❖ ❖ ❖

It felt like the first day of spring. The gentle sloping mountains were a soft green hue, revealing the tree's winter labor. I sat outside talking with a student.

"You know, Mr. Foster, I think you're the best professor I have ever had."

I had apparently pulled off the scholar bit. "I'm not sure if that's a compliment of me or a criticism of your education."

"No. No, my education was fine. You just brought something else. You seemed to care about us. You took an interest in our lives."

His words were shocking. I had worked so hard to be a competent professor, and yet what had mattered most, at least to him, was my time and interest. His words opened up for me a whole new way of thinking about people, service and even education.

Sometimes my awareness lays dormant, waiting for the right time to shake loose meaning from past experiences. Dad had taken interest in my life, and afraid as I was to admit it, his caring had meant a lot. I was beginning to see ways that his presence had helped to shape the person I had become. For ten years, my dad had showed up. He had listened and tried to be involved. He had seldom offered advice and had been quick with a laugh. I had felt accepted and free to be myself without judgment. Dad had offered what Henri Nouwen described as "hospitality," and I realized that this is the finest gift a father can give his son.

I also learned that my dad's kindness had not been isolated to just me. Dad's friend Bill Vaswig described to me with teary eyes how my father had flown across the country to sit with his children in a hospital waiting room during each of Bill's many heart surgeries. I have watched my father serve my mother, going out of his way to care for her and give of himself. I suspect that many of us who are close to him have been touched by his dependable presence in our lives. He's far from perfect, but he's always consistent. When all is said and done, what makes my father great is not his writing or charismatic presence; it is his capacity to love others.

❖ ❖ ❖

Before I invited Dad to hike mountains with me, I had become comfortable with the idea that we wouldn't know each other on any significant level. What transpired, then, had come as a great surprise. On mostly barren and harsh mountain peaks, our relational chasm had been erased. My father gave me permission to dream. He taught me to work. The mountains were the classroom. I discovered that my dad's serious, gentle softness, the qualities I had most disliked, became the qualities I most admire and now try to emulate. I learned that we have remarkable similarities, and that this is good. I am proud to be my father's son.

This world is too dark and lonely not to spend my efforts reaching out and taking risks to get to know others. I now believe that building and cultivating relationships is the most important thing I will ever do. I pray I never lose touch with the hearts of my children. Yet if I do, I hope I will have the insight to see it and the courage and energy to do something about it.

One day when my father is dead and gone, I would like to climb in Colorado with my children and grandchildren. Carrying Dad's heavy stick, I will tell exaggerated tales of scaling these mountains with a slow, old man named Wisdom Chaser. With great fondness, I will tell how much my father loved these mountains. I will tell how we laughed and talked, and how much he loved me.

AFTERWORD
LESSONS FROM THE FINAL FOURTEENER

WHAT NATE HAS WRITTEN ABOUT in these pages did indeed happen. If anything, he has understated the events. Of course, the stories recounted here are only a small sample of our hiking and climbing and backpacking together.

Nate is now far removed from the Rocky Mountains doing what he does best—teaching college. Our days of regular, intensive hiking together have ended. It was something given to us for a season and that season is over. Do I miss it? Fiercely.

You may be wondering what I learned from our decade or more of hiking the Colorado mountains together. What did Nate teach me? What did I feel as a father? These are questions that are difficult to answer adequately.

It was a delight to have our roles reversed. Nate was my teacher in all things wild. I may have never learned to tie those knots, but I learned much about living simply, about traveling light and about contentment with whatever is around me. I learned about prudent risks, about facing fear, about high-altitude climbing. I had great pride in a son who knew so much about surviving and thriving in a wilderness environment.

I learned how little I know about the mysteries of the human equation. And how difficult it is to unlock those mysteries. Struggling up a mountainside together, crossing a swift river lashed to each other, lying in sleeping bags looking up in perfect silence at the stars—for us, these experiences forged the key that ever so slowly began to unlock the hidden chambers of the heart.

I learned that human relationships are delicate and need constant nurturing. I learned that listening with the heart is a gift of grace and something to be treasured. I learned that the bonds of friendship are of greater value than most anything I can think of.

Still, it is not really possible to answer fully the questions about what I learned or what I felt. Something gets stuck in my throat every time I try to articulate an answer. I guess some realities go deeper than words.

❖   ❖   ❖

Nate's skills in wilderness survival are exceptional. He has taken courses in it, studied it intently and led groups of at-risk teenagers into the wilderness . . . and back again.

Nate is incredibly patient in teaching wilderness skills to the uninitiated. Preferring an ultralight tarp to a tent, Nate would try to instruct me in how to secure the tarp so the wind wouldn't whisk it away and the rain wouldn't soak me at night. Patiently he would repeat these instructions to me. Again and again. I must confess: it never took. I'm committed to using my tent.

In backpacking parlance, Nate would be considered a "minimalist." Me, I'm just the opposite, wanting to pack for every possible eventuality. For our first backpacking trek, I was showing Nate what I was planning to take, hoping to get his approval of my foresight into wilderness survival. I had everything spread out all over the living room floor. I remember holding up an extra pair of laces for my boots and a spare buckle for my pack. You know, just in case. Nate smiled and nodded, saying nothing. He, of course, knew I would not need them, but he still let me pack them in . . . and pack them out. Today, some thirteen years later, I am still using the original laces that came with my boots (although the ends are now sealed with duct tape) and the original buckle for my pack!

My tendency to over-pack finally became my undoing on the last fourteener climb Nate and I did together. (At least the heavy pack is where I would like to place the blame!) On one of Nate's trips back to Colorado, we were hoping to summit three rugged peaks which are the most remote of the fourteeners: Windom Peak, Mount Eolus and Sunlight Peak. Taken together, they are the zenith of the Colorado fourteener experience. Windom is a class 2 climb, well within my skill level. Eolus, named after "Aeolus," the Greek god of the winds, is a class 3. The challenging parts are the wild winds and intense thunderstorms that coalesce around Eolus—this massive monarch was certainly well named! Still, I had done class 3 mountains before and felt I could climb it. Sunlight Peak was another story altogether. It is a class 4 or class 5 climb, depending on the route you take. Even the class 4 route has an exposed gap near the summit that you must straddle, and you can peer down the north face between your legs. Gerry Roach's authoritative guidebook says of this exposed leap onto the summit, "If the term *hardest* hinges on the difficulty of a single move, then Sunlight can be called Colorado's hardest fourteener." To say the least, this was far beyond my comfort zone.

◆　◆　◆

We decide to focus our efforts on Windom Peak; after that, we will decide whether to try the other two. The word *Windom* means nothing to me, so I do a little research and discover that it was named after a nineteenth-century politician who most certainly never climbed the mountain and probably never even saw it. That bothers us both sufficiently, and we take it upon ourselves to rename this magnificent mountain "Wisdom."

Reaching the summit of a fourteener is an incomparable experience. The beauty is so mystifying, so surreal, so grand. The hike is an effort, to be sure, but it is also a grace, almost a mercy. It makes the climb utterly gratifying. Somehow with its new name, "Wisdom Peak," this mountain seems worthy of our best effort.

The trailhead for these isolated fourteeners is far removed from any road. Fortunately, we can get there by means of an 1880 Narrow Gauge Railway that is still in operation, running May through October from Durango to the mountain mining town of Silverton. We buy tickets and board the vintage steam locomotive, which twists its way through the Animas River Gorge into the heart of Colorado's Weminuche Wilderness. At about the halfway point, the train makes a backcountry whistlestop and deposits us and our packs at the Needle Creek trailhead. As the Narrow Gauge chugs past us, a couple tourists on their way to Silverton shout out of the window, "Watch out for bears!"

Hmm, a rather disconcerting thought . . . but we are committed now. We shoulder our packs and move out at a fairly good clip (at least for me). Soon, however, the weight of the pack and the elevation gain begin to conspire against me. I didn't weigh my pack (as I normally do), so I have no idea its actual weight, but it feels like a ton. My pace begins to slow considerably. My seasoned plan of finding a pace I can live with, and staying with it, is eluding me. No pace seems slow enough. Patiently, Nate waits for me, pretending to catch his breath.

Our plan is to pack in and set up a base camp at timberline—roughly 11,200 feet. From there we will use daypacks, and in two or three days hope to summit our triple destinations. By the second day, however, it is clear that I am in trouble. I am taking far too long to reach base camp. And when I do get there, will I still have the energy to summit our chosen goals? Nate recognizes the telltale signs of my struggling. He stops, and in a most offhanded manner suggests a change of plan—he obviously has been thinking this out for some time. "Suppose," he says casually, "we abandon the idea of summiting these fourteeners and instead go down to a more tolerable elevation at nearby Mesa Verde National Park and hike the remainder of our time among the cliff dwellings there."

Ugh! Abandon all hopes of bagging a potential three fourteeners! Recognize the limitations of my six-decade-old body! Admit that the mountain has defeated me! How dare Nate even suggest such a thing! And yet . . . So I fast and pray for about five seconds and heartily agreed to his plan. We find a delightful site to camp for the night, up a tributary stream. Exploring the area, we come upon an old miner's outhouse—a comfy one-seater that I try out.

By the next afternoon we are back at the Narrow Gauge pick-up spot and off to the national park. Serendipitously, this is the centennial year for Mesa Verde. In the winter of 1888, two cowboys were riding across the mesa top in search of stray cattle when, through the blowing snow, they saw what to them looked like "a magnificent city" in the canyon below. They were looking at what we today call "Cliff Palace," the largest cliff dwelling in North America. By the early twentieth century, the idea of a national park on this site was conceived. There was only one problem. This area was part of the Puebloan Nation—reservation land set aside for these descendants of the ancestral cliff dwellers when it was assumed that the land was worthless. But now these magnificent cliff dwellings had been found—an archaeologist's gold mine!

A plan was devised to solve the dilemma: the United States government would give to the Puebloan people (archaeologists formerly used the term "Anasazi" until they learned that this was a Navajo word meaning "ancient enemy") two acres for every acre they took to establish Mesa Verde National Park. There was only one small hitch: the transaction was done on geological maps which the Puebloan people did not understand, and every acre "given" to them was already part of their existing reservation. The contemporary term for this is "a swindle."

Anyway, because this is the centennial year for the park, numerous sites that hitherto had been closed to the public are now open for exploring. At seven thousand feet elevation and with a light daypack, I am in my element. Together Nate and I trek many a mile to ancient cliff dwellings and stunning petroglyphs and pictographs that have not been seen by the public since the park's founding. I gaze at these ancient etchings and paintings on the cliff sides for a long time, trying hard to extract meaning from them. Nate, ever the iconoclast, sees them merely as an ancient expression of graffiti. Although it does not appear in the Mesa Verde rock carvings (but in every store and shop for miles around), I am especially intrigued by the well-known Kokopelli image, dubbed by popular tradition as "the flute player." Nate quickly pops my esoteric bubble by informing me that the consensus of archaeological research now suggests that what is in Kokopelli's hands is not a flute at all but part of his own anatomy . . . an early example of soft-core pornography, perhaps. I guess there really is nothing new under the sun!

At the end of each of the park ranger talks (which were quite good, I might add), they welcome questions. Nate, totally without recrimination or reproach, always seems to find a way to ask if the Park Service has ever considered returning the land to the Puebloan people. He raises this issue ever so gently and utterly without reprisal.

Watching this, I find Nate's persistent nudge of social justice quite appropriate. And quite revealing. I watch the various rangers handle his query in rather different ways. One is defensive, another retreats into legalese, and still another frankly admits that the deal to establish the park was clearly a swindle and that some kind of reparations would be in order. But no one ever even mentions returning the land to these descendants of the ancestral cliff dwellers.

Returning home, I am sobered by my physical limitations but glad for our adventure together, Nate and me. And while I did not summit "Wisdom Peak," I did learn that in life we are ever chasing wisdom.

❖ ❖ ❖

I now hike the mountains and canyons of the Colorado Rockies mostly by myself. As I do I remember well a special time, sacred even, given to father and son. I remember . . . I remember.

Richard J. Foster

ACKNOWLEDGMENTS

I REMAIN AMAZED AT THE interconnectedness of us all. It's foolish to think I can accomplish anything independent of the ideas, encouragement and help of others. I owe a deep gratitude to the many who helped shape this project.

Dad, for being crazy enough to follow me up a mountain and allowing me to share our adventures with the world, for better or worse.

Mom, for trusting that I wouldn't get Dad killed and always being cool with him spending weekends wandering through the woods with me. I have grown to appreciate you in so many ways.

Terry Hedrick and my friends at Church of the Savior, for teaching me what a Christian community can look like. Your simple congregation is so beautiful. The years I spent with you meant so much, I never should have left.

Chris Wilgers, for helping me unpack this mess.

Tim Davis, for teaching me how to suffer well. Your expectations force me to dream. You remain an exceptional man.

To my friends at the Erie Friday night group.

Matt Larime, for all the adventures we shared.

Nancy Arnold, for spending an hour in my face demanding that I write a book. It took over seven years, but here it is. You know you really freaked me out!

Jan Harris, for casting the vision.

Kathy Helmers, for taking a chance on me.

Cindy Bunch, for walking me through this process. Your approach was exactly what I needed. You're the best!

Bob Fields and my friends at CleftRock, for giving me a much-needed place to work. Your love for Todd inspires me at many levels.

Tim Cooper, for your enthusiasm, friendship and detailed critiques.

Pat Bailey, for allowing me to slack on my academic duties.

Paul Patton, your life-giving encouragement was needed.

Patricia Burbank, for journeying with me.

Sigur Rós and the group The Album Leaf, your tunes filled the air with wonder and creativity, giving me room to think.

Bono, brother, you know your poetry was the soundtrack of my writing.

Henry Rollins, for keeping me honest.

Malcom Smith, for understanding so much.

❖　❖　❖

Autumn Hope Foster, you are the best daughter I could have ever hoped for! I don't think you realize just how courageous of a girl you are. Daily I find encouragement from your beautiful smile. You had to give so much for this project. Thank you! Your love for words and well-scripted phrases reminded me of the joy of writing. You'll be happy to know that our reading times together worked their way into this project. You will find the voices of Ingalls Wilder, Twain, Lewis, Burnett, Tolkien and Warner lodged within these pages.

Kyren Nathaniel Foster, I've been working on this project for your entire life. And though you may not know it, you too have had to give much. When I begin to take myself too seriously, you bring me back to reality with your collapsing hugs, playful spirit and obsession with potty humor. The way you look at me forces me to be a better person. I have a feeling that one day you will have to extend patience to me on the trail as I did for my father. You're the best son I ever could have hoped for!

My wife, Christy, I am significantly indebted to you in many ways. From the very beginning to the bitter end, your engagement, grace and vision shaped so much of this book. Only you know just how hard this whole process was, much of that burden you had to bear. I can't think about the sacrifices you have made without tearing up. Thanks for believing in me—I remain frightened by all you see in me. You know you touch my soul. . . . How about we try a few more years together?

Nathan and Richard

Ziggy, 1995-2007

A more intuitive, compassionate and
loving dog I will never know.

LIKEWISE. *Go and do.*

A man comes across an ancient enemy, beaten and left for dead. He lifts the wounded man onto the back of a donkey and takes him to an inn to tend to the man's recovery. Jesus tells this story and instructs those who are listening to "go and do likewise."

Likewise books explore a compassionate, active faith lived out in real time. When we're skeptical about the status quo, Likewise books challenge us to create culture responsibly. When we're confused about who we are and what we're supposed to be doing, Likewise books help us listen for God's voice. When we're discouraged by the troubled world we've inherited, Likewise books encourage us to hold onto hope.

In this life we will face challenges that demand our response. Likewise books face those challenges with us so we can act on faith.

likewisebooks.com